The book you hold in your hands is more pow[er]... illuminating than you assume, more transforma[...]... are weak-kneed or faint of heart, drop it and run. If you're happy... cent or content to live on autopilot, turn back now. Because this book will change the way you see everything. *The Sacred Enneagram* is not a just book about an ancient personality framework with a funny name. It is a roadmap to self-understanding written by one of the great spiritual practitioners of my generation. Read it now and you can thank me later.

–**Jonathan Merritt,** contributing writer for *The Atlantic* and author of *Learning to Speak God from Scratch*

The gentleness of Chris's tone mixed with the truth in these pages makes this book unavoidable for anyone who not only cares about their own mental and spiritual well-being but also wants to see others flourish.

–**Propaganda,** spoken word poet and activist

Integrated within these pages is Chris's extensive knowledge and understanding of this ancient tool, along with depth in his teaching of contemplative spirituality as practiced by Jesus. Readers are offered a powerful way forward in their unique journey of spiritual transformation through aligning Christian contemplative prayer postures to specific Enneagram types.

–**Nina M. Barnes,** Dean of Spiritual Formation & Leadership, University of Northwestern–St. Paul

The Sacred Enneagram is a groundbreaking contribution to the Enneagram community, providing unique spiritual growth insights for all nine types. If you're not yet convinced of the value, depth, and accuracy of the Enneagram, Chris demystifies and makes this ancient wisdom more accessible than ever.

–**George Mekhail,** pastor, The Riverside Church NYC

Understanding the Enneagram is not just an exercise in secular self-discovery but a journey toward living out rhythms of rest and reflection that will lead to deep spiritual growth. By grounding the Enneagram in the core truth of Scripture's teachings about ourselves and God, this book helps us live into the full promise of who God created us to be, with impact on the communities and places God has called us to serve. I applaud Chris for doing the hard work of grounding an age-old practice into such practical and wise applications for those of us who seek to honor God in all of who we are and all of what we do.

–**Jenny Yang,** Vice President of Advocacy and Policy, World Relief

Through years of careful research and mindful study, Chris uses the Enneagram to illuminate the best and the worst of us and shine a light down the path to our truest selves. *The Sacred Enneagram* will find you when you need to be found.

–**Orenda Fink,** singer-songwriter

The Sacred Enneagram beautifully integrates the journey of self-discovery with guidelines that are simultaneously seasoned and filled with childlike wonder, personal and inviting. Instead of wandering around a hall of mirrors that most self-discovery texts build, *The Sacred Enneagram* walks with you through holy ground and fills you with love and life that ultimately pours out and must be shared.

–**Alex Hwang,** vocalist of Run River North

As the years pass, I often find myself asking, "Who am I?" *The Sacred Enneagram* is a book that I will forever use as a guide throughout my lifelong journey of self-discovery.

–**Shirley Chung,** "Top Chef" finalist and restauranteur

Accessible to the spiritual journey of any seeker, Chris Heuertz beautifully translates this simple truth: that God is accessible when we know ourselves deeply. *The Sacred Enneagram* helps us to learn how to take that deep dive into our own essence to find the Divine.

–**Mona Haydar,** rapper, poet, activist, theologian

The Sacred Enneagram is a fascinating exploration into our inherent and undiscovered gifts of humanity. Learning about the Enneagram has awakened my understanding of Self in connection to God, my reactive tendencies in leadership, and hopeful opportunities for growth, discernment and spiritual formation. Learning about the Enneagram has expanded my heart's capacity for compassion—toward those I fail to understand and especially toward myself.

–**Nikole Lim,** Cofounder and International Director,
Freely in Hope

This is the Enneagram book we've all been waiting for—what to do next, once you uncover your type—and Chris Heuertz is the perfect guide for the journey. His work with me on the Enneagram has been nothing short of transformative.

–**Kirsten Powers,** CNN political analyst, *USA Today* columnist,
and recovering One

The SACRED ENNEAGRAM

Finding Your Unique Path to Spiritual Growth

CHRISTOPHER L. HEUERTZ

ZONDERVAN

The Sacred Enneagram
Copyright © 2017 by Christopher L. Heuertz

Requests for information should be addressed to:
Zondervan, 3900 Sparks Dr. SE, Grand Rapids, Michigan 49546

ISBN 978-0-310-34827-6 (softcover)

ISBN 978-0-310-34815-3 (ebook)

All Scripture quotations are taken from *The Inclusive Bible*, © 2007 by Priests for Equality. Published in the United States by Rowman and Littlefield Publisher, Inc. All rights reserved.

Any internet addresses (websites, blogs, etc.) and telephone numbers in this book are offered as a resource. They are not intended in any way to be or imply an endorsement by Zondervan, nor does Zondervan vouch for the content of these sites and numbers for the life of this book.

Author is represented by Christopher Ferebee, Attorney and Literary Agent, www .christopherferebee.com

Cover design: Charles Brock | Faceout Studio
Cover illustrations: Shutterstock®
Author photo: Scott Drickey
Interior illustrations: Elnora Turner
Interior design: Kait Lamphere

First printing July 2017 / Printed in the United States of America

20 21 PC/LSCH 15

I dedicate this work to my teachers:

Marion,

Russ,

Helen,

Richard,

I honor you.

Contents

PART III: Finding Your Unique
Path to Spiritual Growth

Foreword

by Father Richard Rohr

> As long as you do not have experience
> of *this dying and becoming*, you are only
> a troubled guest on this dark earth.

JOHANN WOLFGANG VON GOETHE

I was taught the Enneagram by my own Jesuit spiritual director in Cincinnati, Ohio, in 1973. I noticed Father Jim O'Brien was often getting to the heart of the matter with me rather quickly, and he was so insightful that one would have thought he had known me for a long time—or on some occasions, as if he knew me better than I knew myself. I thought he surely had the rare gift of "reading souls."

But the even better part was that he made me feel so good about what I thought were clearly my faults. And even seeing those faults that I thought were very well hidden. How? And then he could often see my best in what I thought was my worst. He was like everybody's perfect dream friend.

I could see my spiritual director was not naïve or trying to please me, nor did he romanticize my eager personality; he simply got me to look at things in a much broader and less judgmental way, which as a type One on the Enneagram is a major victory. He allowed me to see myself in a way that was devastatingly true and humiliating at the same time. Yet strangely comforting too.

I could not deny either the truth or the humiliation of what I was seeing in myself, yet it was given in such an indirect, persuasive, and compassionate way that I had no trouble saying a slow yes to what I was hearing and feeling. But I do remember my ego rebelling and already planning strategies to avoid detection as a One by anyone else. As if I could. They probably already knew.

I remember driving back to the Franciscan friary where I lived, staring straight ahead, and I am sure I looked like a deer caught in the headlights—when the truth of it all came crashing down in my mind. *Oh, my God, I went to the seminary for the wrong reason; I was a "good boy" for the wrong reason; I obeyed the laws of God, church, and parents for the wrong reason; I became celibate for the wrong reason; and now I am trying to save the world with my endless "zeal" for the wrong reason.* On and on I berated myself. I had not learned Jim's compassion yet. That would take years.

But my self-discovery continued at various levels for the next years. I soon saw that many people who loved or admired me actually loved me for my faults: my righteous zeal and being so serious and conscientious. And many people who disliked or resented me did it for what I had always thought were my very virtues. No one likes a "goody two shoes," a little Boy Scout, an adult who grew up way too quickly, someone overly punctual, a "perfectionist" but only in one or two select areas—so not really a perfectionist at all. Only where I can sort of "pull it off" successfully! I am still uncovering these humiliations—and the grace that follows them—to this day, and I am now in my seventy-fifth year.

The difference is that now I am not humiliated by my own humiliation, nor am I inflated by the reports from my own self-congratulation society. God has honestly taught me to smile and say,

"What can you expect from little Richard?" Not out of disgust or shame anymore, but only out of liberating and healing self-knowledge. Now I have little to prove and little to protect. And the wisdom of the Enneagram has been a major part of my journey toward inner freedom.

It led me to writing books on "the True Self," giving talks on growth and change, and specializing in shadow work first in myself, but then in church, culture, and history. My gift became my curse and yet it is still my greatest gift, and it seems that I cannot have one without the other.

One knows oneself only at the price of one's innocence.

Chris Heuertz, my dear friend and confidant, has gone on his own similar journey, and I am most happy to recommend this excellent book on the Enneagram to you. You will find here some excellent content, many new insights, and the compassion that genuine spirituality always provides—which I know Chris lives personally and now hands on to you.

You will not be the same after you read this book. You will surely be happier. We do not need any more "troubled guests on this dark earth."

Richard Rohr, OFM
Center for Action and Contemplation

PART I

WHAT IS *the* ENNEAGRAM?

1

The Question *of* Identity

Exploring Who We Are, How We Got Lost,
and How We Might Find Our Way Back
Home to Our True Identity

For the last decade, I've been meeting with Father Larry Gillick for spiritual direction. He is one of the most perceptive people I've known. He's a scrappy old Irish-American Jesuit priest, and sometimes as I'm leaving his office on Creighton University's campus, he'll affectionately say, "Sometimes you just need a good butt-kicking."

He once told me the story of a visit he made to a local Catholic elementary school. After sharing with a group of the students, a young girl—probably third or fourth grade—approached him and struck up a conversation. A few moments into their discussion, a look of pure astonishment flashed in the student's eyes.

Suddenly, she blurted out, "You're blind!" Which is true. Due to a sickness, he lost his sight when he was just a small child.

With genuine tenderness, Father Gillick responded, "That's not news to me."

But before he could say anything else, she quickly moved from shock to sadness, replying, "You don't know what you look like."

That profound statement from such a young person caught Father

Gillick off guard, and before he could comment she softly said, "You're beautiful."

I'm deeply moved every time I think about that little exchange. It's a very *human* story in which many of us can find our *own* story tucked inside. When it comes to recognizing the truth of our own identities, most of us experience a symbolic version of blindness that keeps us from seeing ourselves for who we really are.

We live unawakened lives marked by self-perpetuating lies about who we think we are—or how we wish to be seen. Tragically, we don't know who we are or what we look like. And often, it takes an unlikely "other" to remind us what's true—*you're beautiful.*

Each and every one of us is beautiful. Each and every one of us is beloved by God.

From this starting point we can begin an honest interrogation of the depths of our identity, of who we really are. When we accept our inherent beauty, we find the courage to examine what makes us beautiful—to honestly encounter both the good and the bad, the shadow and the light.

More than anything I've encountered, the Enneagram helps us do just that. It exposes the lies we tell ourselves about our identities. It helps us realize there's much to learn about who we can become. It illuminates what's good and true and beautiful about each of us.

IDENTITY AND DIGNITY

More and more I'm convinced that the paramount question plaguing humanity has to do with identity.

Who am I? This is the fundamental question of our human experience, the one that compels us to search for meaning.

Every time I meet someone, I try to listen to the subtext, the meaning behind the words they use to introduce themselves.

Often our first interaction with a new acquaintance exposes our fears or insecurities, demonstrated in how we describe ourselves. Usually we allow carefully curated fragments of our identities to lay claim to the whole.

I'm frequently guilty of beginning my own introductions with references to what I've *done* or *do* for a living, as if that tells someone who I *am*. "Hey, I'm Chris. I spent twenty years with an international humanitarian organization fighting human trafficking; I currently run a nonprofit, a center for contemplative activism." These little bits of my story that I lead with only bolster my overidentification with the lies I've come to believe about who I think I am. I constantly have to remind myself that I am more than the good (or the bad) I've done in my life, that in fact, I'm much more than what I've done, what I have, and what others think about me. These fragments of the whole are only small parts of my identity, not the entirety of who I truly am.

But what do we mean by identity? The missiologist-theologians Vinay Samuel and Chris Sugden, who have studied identity and dignity, nuance the differences between the two as those of *substance* and *value*, suggesting, "Identity answers the question 'Who am I?', while dignity answers the question, 'What am I worth?'"[1]

Seems so simple.

Makes such sense.

Within our historic Christian faith we affirm that all humanity bears the imprint of the Divine, that we are made in the image of God. This is the starting point for drawing forward our sense of dignity, the intrinsic value that is *ascribed* not *earned*, based on our essence in reflecting a good and loving God.

If we can start with the grace of resting in our dignity, then the truth of our identity flows forward. "While identity must not be confused with dignity, dignity in a Christian view assumes identity."[2]

Tragically, most of us start with our sense of identity, believing that if we build out the mythology of who we think we are, then the more attractive our identity and the more valuable we become. But when we equate our dignity with the sum value of the fortification of stories we tell about our identity, we create a no-win scenario that will always lead to disillusionment and pain. Overidentifying with our success or failure, allowing the fragments of our identity to lay claim to the whole, and falling into the addictive loop of our mental and emotional preoccupations keep us stuck. This is what entrenches the illusions of our ego's mythologies.

This is how we get ourselves lost. The challenge is to find our way home.

My own consistent struggle is to recognize my addictive tendency to validate my worth (dignity) by curating an unrealistic and unattainable projection of who I think I need to be (identity). By pandering to thin or worn-out versions of my False Self, I've fallen into the trap that Franciscan priest and author Father Richard Rohr (hereafter, Father Richard) often warns about: "Every unrealistic expectation is a resentment waiting to happen." And as I constantly fail to meet my own standards, the resentment keeps me trapped.

The Three Lies We Let Define Us

When I get stuck trying to untangle the confusion around my notions of self, I frequently return to Father Henri Nouwen's classic teaching on identity.

Henri Nouwen was a Dutch Catholic priest who had an incredibly accomplished academic career that began with a visiting professorship at the University of Notre Dame. He also was one of the twentieth century's foremost Christian spirituality writers, authoring thousands of pages of instant and timeless classics.

In the early 1980s he left a teaching position at Yale Divinity

School to reassess his own vocation. He felt somehow that God was igniting a repurposing of his life's work, a calling to serve and live among people in poverty. So he moved to South America where he spent six months learning Spanish in Bolivia before serving as a priest among the oppressed of Peru. But as he discerned what the proper "yes" was to this evolving vocation, he determined it didn't involve staying in South America.

So Nouwen returned to the United States where he took a teaching job at Harvard Divinity School. It was during this period of his life, while on a silent retreat in Chicago (coincidentally facilitated by my spiritual director, Father Larry Gillick), that he first met community members from L'Arche, an international group of communities for adults with intellectual disabilities.

From those introductions, Nouwen ended up meeting L'Arche's founder, Jean Vanier. Through their sacred friendship, Nouwen began to find direction for his inner restlessness. Vanier's example of embodied solidarity and love, rooted in community, provoked a refreshed vocational imagination that captivated him.

Nouwen invited Vanier to visit Harvard to deliver a series of lectures titled "From Brokenness to Community." Vanier was astounded at how well loved Nouwen was by his students yet how dissatisfied he seemed to be in an academic setting. Shortly after, Vanier invited Nouwen to join L'Arche first in France and then, later on, in Canada.

After finally settling into community outside Toronto, Nouwen hit a psychological wall. Suddenly he was part of a community where the vast majority of its core members would never have passed the admissions process for any of the universities he taught at, let alone be able to pick up and read many of his books. Unlike in years past, Nouwen could no longer hide behind his academic and publishing successes; the core members of his new community weren't impressed by any of it. In fact, it really didn't matter if he was their new priest or their new janitor; he was just Henri to them. But who was "Henri" to Henri?

Long before, Nouwen had lost himself by allowing some of his professional successes to claim the whole of his identity. Nouwen didn't really know who he was apart from those accomplishments. In his new community, the scaffolding of his disordered identity came crashing down all around him.

I first came across Nouwen's journey of rediscovering the truth of his identity while watching some old VHS tapes in the mid-1990s, recordings of three talks he gave at the Crystal Cathedral in Southern California. The gist was simple: Nouwen suggested we all find ourselves bouncing around three very human lies that we believe about our identity: *I am what I have*, *I am what I do*, and *I am what other people say or think about me.*[*]

The teaching resonated deeply with me. I was in my early twenties still trying to figure out who I was. I had some early success in my activist career by helping start South Asia's first pediatric AIDS care home for children either born HIV positive or orphaned because of the disease. Before turning twenty-five I became the executive director of an international humanitarian organization, and I had even spent time with Mother Teresa during the last few years of her life. Back then, I latched onto all these successful pieces of my story.

Furthermore, in lieu of not having earned a graduate degree (something I felt some insecurity about), I parlayed my professional achievements into a sort of vocational credibility.

In a large sense, I believed I was what I *had*—a beautiful wife and a happy marriage, a stable community, and a fulfilling job.

---

[*] These reflections on Nouwen's three lies come from a series of messages entitled "Being the Beloved" which he delivered during appearances on Crystal Cathedral Ministries' *Hour of Power* television show in 1992.

I believed I was what I *did*—I fought for the vulnerable; I built communities; and I got to travel all over the world doing what I loved.

I believed I was *what other people thought about me*—people saw me as compassionate, deeply rooted in my faith, and ambitious.

Though I had a beautiful life, did meaningful work, and enjoyed fairly positive reviews of it all, those things didn't ultimately define me, nor could they possibly capture the essence of my identity.

Interestingly, as I grew older, my illusions of self were less and less driven by what I had or did or by the good that was said of me. Instead, I gradually became more driven by all that I had failed to do, all that I still wanted, and the negative things people thought and said about me.

Even now, when I'm not centered, I find myself falling to one side or the other of these lies. And I'll bet if you're honest with yourself, all three of these lies lay claim to your sense of identity as well. Each touches on a stress fracture in our ego that we've learned to work around. But when these lies take hold, they don't let go. Instead they fortify the mythology of our personality.

Like many people, I find myself constantly having to untangle myself from these three lies. They're human. They're consistent. And they're powerful.

The Three Programs for Happiness

Another driver that contributes to the disconnect with our True Self is the way we pursue happiness.

During the renewal of contemplative spirituality in the 1960s and 1970s, many Western Christians turned to Eastern methods like Zen meditation to nurture their spirituality. This shift grieved Father Thomas Keating, a Trappist monk from the Cistercian order, who saw curious pilgrims bypass his own Benedictine monastery, oblivious to the fact that the Christian tradition held helpful contemplative practices itself. Consequently, he worked to make Centering Prayer accessible to all, giving a time-honored contemplative practice back to the laity.

In his writings, Father Keating speaks of consistent contemplative practice as a way to rest in the grace of our being. Keating also emphasizes that contemplative practice helps us wake up to the truth of ourselves. His framework for understanding the process of breaking free into our True Self is a psychological developmental overlay of our inner landscape that he calls "programs for happiness."

Keating explains that as children we all need an appropriate amount of *power and control, affection and esteem,* and *security and survival* for healthy psychological grounding. But as we mature, our tendency is to *overidentify* with one of these programs for happiness, keeping us developmentally and spiritually stuck.

Keating suggests, "Without adequate fulfillment of these biological needs, we probably would not survive infancy. Since the experience of the presence of God is not there at the age we start to develop self-consciousness, these three instinctual needs are all we have with which to build a program for happiness. Without the help of reason to modify them, we build a universe with ourselves at the center, around which all human faculties revolve like planets around the sun."[3]

It's important to remember that power and control, affection and esteem, and security and survival aren't bad needs in and of themselves. The problem arises when in our adult lives we become addicted to one of these programs to maintain our happiness. The word *addiction* comes from the Latin *addico,* which suggests being literally given over to something in devotion. As the term evolved, it took on the legal connotation of enslavement as a form debt. While we need these programs for happiness to foster healthy development, once enslaved to them we are their debtor, paying with our lost identity.

So how have we gotten so far off track? How do we heal ourselves from the false identities we've reinforced? Ultimately, how do we find our way home to the God of love and our true identity?

This is where the Enneagram comes in. It reveals our path for recovering our true identity and helps us navigate the journey home to God.

2

What Is the Enneagram?

Learning the Essentials of This Ancient Tool

Often misunderstood as simply a personality tool to describe quirks and traits of people's individuality, the Enneagram goes much further than mere caricatures. The contemporary Enneagram of Personality* illustrates the nine ways we get lost, but also the nine ways we can come home to our True Self. Put another way, it exposes nine ways we lie to ourselves about who we think we are, nine ways we can come clean about those illusions, and nine ways we can find our way back to God.

The Enneagram is much more than just another popular formula to pair people to the collection of their personality foibles and eccentricities. It explains the "why" of how we think, act, and feel. It helps us come to terms with our gifts as well as the addictive patterns

---

* Historically there are several versions of the Enneagram. In fact, Óscar Ichazo (the Bolivian wisdom teacher who developed the Enneagram most commonly used today) taught 108 different Enneagons (as he called them). Today, the most popular versions of the Enneagram include the Sufi Enneagram, the Enneagram of Process, the Harmony Enneagram, and the Gurdjieffian Enneagram, but I will be drawing attention specifically to the Enneagram of Personality, which reveals nine types of human character structure.

that tether us to our greatest interpersonal, spiritual, and emotional challenges. The Enneagram invites us to deeper self-awareness as a doorway to spiritual growth.

When we can find the courage to be honest with ourselves, we're ready for the Enneagram, for the Enneagram exposes the illusions that have defined our sense of self. In this way, the Enneagram may be the most effective tool for personal liberation. By revealing our illusions, the Enneagram emphasizes the urgency of inner work—the intentional focus required to prioritize the nurturing of our spirituality by facing pain from our past, exploring areas where we've neglected emotional healing, and consciously* examining our struggle to bring our best self forward in our vocation, relationships, and faith.

Unfortunately, we soon realize that most of the inner work is painfully mundane; there's sort of a bland, everyday, humdrum monotony about it. In fact, much of the inner work can be boiled down to faithful contemplative prayer practice. Though it's critical, there's nothing exciting about quietly and faithfully making time on a daily basis for meditation. And so part of us always resists this important piece of our personal journey home.

Ultimately, though, for those willing to persevere, the Enneagram offers a sacred map for our souls; a map that, when understood, leads us home to our true identity and to God.

It reminds me of the opening scene from the film *The Wizard of*

---

* When referring to the conscious mind, the subconscious, and the unconscious, I am delineating the notion of the three minds or three of the basic ways our egos operate. The *conscious* is what we experience as awareness of the present, most attainable through thoughts and the intellect. A layer below our conscious mind lies the *subconscious*, our awareness and memories that we are not attentive to in the present but that are still accessible through triggers, familiar sensations, or intentional recall—in this way, most attainable through our feelings and emotions. At the base of all the levels of consciousness is the *unconscious* as that which is largely consciously inaccessible on an instinctual level yet still drives attitudes and behaviors, often felt more in the body than in the mind or emotions. Contemplative practice is one of the most effective ways of engaging and integrating these three levels of consciousness. When we develop contemplative practices, we grow in awareness of the lack of integration within our egos so that we can learn to self-observe, which ultimately allows for self-correction.

Oz, a classic American movie that many of us have seen more times than we can remember.

After the film's initial credits scroll across the screen, the viewer is introduced to a young Kansas farm girl, Dorothy Gale, and her little dog Toto. They're running away from home down a dusty old country trail cutting through the plains of middle America—a significant image that sets up the rest of the adventure on the parallel path of her unconscious dream: the magical Yellow Brick Road.

Like Dorothy, we're all trying to find our way home. We're all looking for ways to get back to our True Self.

As the opening scene unfolds we quickly learn that Toto has been on the neighbor's property, chasing Miss Almira Gulch's cat. Almira has had enough. She's so fed up that she's obtained permission from the county sheriff to euthanize little Toto. Flustered by it all, Dorothy takes an aggressive stance defending Toto, willing to put up a fight for his mischievous behavior.

Dorothy's response is a lot like our addictive tendencies to defend our own illusions, enabling our ego to maintain its control over our sensibilities and emotional states.

I imagine Dorothy's little dog Toto as a representation of her inner critic, always yapping about something, constantly snapping and trying to bite others, and perpetually restless. We all have it, this cardinal component of our subconscious. Our inner critic is that part of ourselves that we turn into the pet that needs our constant attention and routine feeding. The inner critic is what gets us in trouble from time to time and continually resists the invitation to the task of our inner work. It's one of the many techniques we use to keep ourselves asleep or to help us cope with the pain we don't want to face, ensuring we stay stuck in our addictive tendencies to remain tethered to our False Self.

And this False Self of ours doesn't need more help in keeping us asleep in our illusions. Again, this is where the Enneagram is an aid to waking up. One of its most helpful aspects is how it exposes nine ways our human nature manages our ego's* collection of coping addictions that we have wrapped around our most intimate and deepest pain—our Childhood Wound. For many of us, these wounds go largely undetected for most of our lives, yet we live unconsciously into the trajectory they set us on. The mental and emotional scar tissues of these wounds form the nine different ways we cope with their pain, molding tragic character flaws we often overidentify with, aiding in the development (or malformation) of our personalities.

The Enneagram teaches us nine patterns of human character structure archetypes. These patterns fortify a kind of whole-person muscle memory (which includes the psychological or mental, emotional or spiritual, and somatic or physical) that shapes how we think, feel, and act.

Simply put, the Enneagram offers nine mirrors for self-reflection. These nine mirrors, if we choose to gaze into them directly, can help us shake loose of our illusions that get us lost from home in the first place.

The nine mirrors are nine types, of which we are dominant in one:

---

* Throughout this work I will refer to the "ego" as one's identity construct rooted in our sense of awareness that vacillates between our conscious sense of self and the subconscious influences that fortify our notions of who we are. Though our ego is a substantial construction of our notion of identity, in large part it is the illusion diverting us from who we can become when awakened through self-awareness and committed contemplative practice. The truth of self is rooted in the instinctive unconscious, the part of us that is almost never uncovered or recognized except when touched by deep love, awakened through deep prayer, or drawn forward through psychoanalysis. Though conscious awareness is required to observe our ego, fundamentally our ego is how our character structure emerges through (but not limited to) nature, preferences and affinities, religious and existential beliefs, talents, abilities, our Childhood Wound, relationships, and connections to institutions and communities. Within religious traditions the idea of our False Self or "sinful nature" has sometimes been compared to the ego (even co-opted as the ego), but I use egoic language in a neutral or indifferent aspect, not making judgment about the sinfulness of the ego, but drawing attention to the ego's tendency toward a lack of awareness.

> ➤ Type One strives for principled excellence as moral duty.

> ➤ Type Two strives for lavish love through self-sacrifice.

> ➤ Type Three strives for appreciative recognition through curated successes.

> ➤ Type Four strives for the discovery of identity for faithful authenticity.

> ➤ Type Five strives for decisive clarity through thoughtful conclusions.

> ➤ Types Six strives for steady constancy through confident loyalty.

> ➤ Type Seven strives for imaginative freedom for inspirational independence.

> ➤ Type Eight strives for impassioned intensity for unfettered autonomy.

> ➤ Type Nine strives for harmonious peacefulness as congruent repose.

THE ENNEAGRAM AS A SACRED MAP

Much of my elementary and secondary education growing up in Omaha, Nebraska, took place in Catholic and Protestant private schools. As a child, both at church and at school, I was taught and retaught stories from Scripture on colorful one-dimensional flannelgraph boards. There was little explicit doctrine fused into the stories (I can imagine the implicit doctrinal slants I must have ingested) until I moved into adolescence, when apologetics and theology entered my religious formation process.

Maybe you've had a similar experience growing up. Understanding the stories from our church or worshiping community lays a foundation for opening our hearts and minds to their underlying principles. The stories are really never about the story; they point to something much deeper and significantly more beautiful than the symbols they contain. These principles of the stories, with their doctrinal implications, lead to the codification of beliefs that ultimately requires systematic theology to be built up around them.

Once the meaning of the stories is internalized and the theological doctrines are integrated into a person's faith identity, people begin embodying their beliefs in a way that speaks for itself in the real world, beyond dogmatic defense with words.

As the most devout believers of any faith tradition mature, they find themselves quietly and undramatically allowing the fruit of their lives to speak for itself more than relying on conversionist tactics. That's truly the fruit of real conversion, when our lives (not our words) validate authentic transformation.

The movement from *basic knowledge* to *principled understanding* to *embodied integration* is the idealized essence of mastery in any growth process—including the Enneagram.

Sure, it doesn't take long for Enneagram enthusiasts to learn their way around the diagram, reciting the conventional descriptors for each of the nine types. It's also not uncommon for students of the Enneagram to move beyond mere recitation of the basics to critical engagement with some of the more sophisticated aspects of the Enneagram. Less common, though still not rare, are the innovative Enneagram devotees who take progressive liberties with the system itself. But it is a peculiar person who *integrates* the illuminations of the Enneagram in a way that obliges less direct reference to the tool because of her or his own internalized command of its deeper meanings. This becomes obvious when suddenly you see how Enneagram types aren't just buckets for unique sets of idiosyncrasies but rather offer clues to the essence of each person's particular purpose.

After all, truth is meant to be lived—in our everyday, embodied lives. But truth can be hard to find when it has been hidden from us for so long behind our personality.

Let's examine this for a moment. The English word *personality* is derived from the Latin word for "mask." Simply put, our personality is the mask we wear. Taking off that mask, trying to get behind the mask, is the work of the spiritual journey.

A mark of spiritual growth is when we stop polishing the mask and instead start working on our character. The Enneagram helps us do that character-structure work. The English word *character* comes from the Greek word meaning "engraving into stone." And that's what we're trying to do here with the help of the Enneagram—to chip away at our being, like the most talented of sculptors, and reveal our soul's essence in its purest form.

Awakening to what the Enneagram exposes within us often leads to an urgent unmasking of our false identity, what has become our personality. Embracing a contemplative approach to working with the Enneagram allows for discernment to develop, and we soon realize that contrary to pop psychology, personality is not fixed. Spiritual growth and transformation are the result of exposing the masks or illusions of personality and getting to the core of identity. The Enneagram supports this inner work.

Pilgrimage of a Soul, written by my wife Phileena, is a moving memoir of what is possible when we prayerfully dare to remove our masks of false identity. Pairing the Enneagram with contemplative spiritual practice helps us make this authentic passage. In *Pilgrimage of a Soul*, Phileena alludes to why the Enneagram is so helpful:

> We are asleep to our unconscious motivations, and these motivations mask our True Self. In essence we are hiding. And the wound in our soul remains unhealed, infecting every aspect of our lives. We are so asleep to our reality that we don't know we are hiding behind the masks of our [F]alse [S]elf. In our slumber we are unable to distinguish between what is true and what is false. These masks become so familiar to us, they become a part of our very identity.

When I awakened to the presence of masks in my life, I knew not at first what was truly me and what was a false version of me. What was a mask and what was authentic, beautiful me? Only time would tell.[1]

We wake up when we stop fueling our own self-preoccupation and allow self-realization to serve as an invitation to deep union with ourselves and God, which naturally leads to solidarity with others. Many people who come across the Enneagram get stuck with the overviews and the thick descriptions of their own type; they love to learn more and more about themselves while resisting the implications of the gift of self-knowledge. The Enneagram is not a tool for self-absorption but instead a map for self-liberation.

When we give ourselves to the hard work of integrating what we have come to learn about ourselves, the Enneagram becomes a sacred map of our soul, one that shows us the places where we have vulnerabilities or tendencies to get stuck as well as the possibilities of where we can go for deeper freedom and inner peace. This sacred map isn't fatalistic; it's not deterministic; it's not a horoscope or a predetermined course that doesn't allow for personalized twists—it's a compassionate sketch of possibilities and opportunities, pointing us back to our True Self and to the anchoring God whose name is Love.

As noted earlier, this sacred map comes to us in nine variations, each a unique rendering of the way we set out on our own inner journey to reconnect with our essential nature. The nine explorations of the soul are pilgrimages unto themselves, consecrated and prayerful voyages with focused intentions.

Each of these nine distinct journeys helps describe the dynamic flow of how our Enneagram type emerges within us.

THE NINE TYPES AND THEIR PRIMARY NEEDS

Though there are quite a few helpful handles for each of the types, I prefer to refer to the nine types by their numbers, specifically suggesting that someone is "dominant in type Two" instead of calling Twos "Givers" or "Helpers," or referring to those "dominant in type Nine" rather than calling Nines "Peacemakers" or "Mediators." Sometimes I'm concerned that the names assigned to each of the types describe their social functions or roles without getting to the *reasons* behind type. So even though they are handy, the familiar names for each type can also be unhelpful, limiting caricatures.

	Riso/Hudson Enneagram Institute	Helen Palmer Enneagram in the Narrative Tradition	Hurley/Dobson Enneagram in the Healing Tradition
Type One	The Reformer	Perfectionist	Achiever
Type Two	The Helper	Giver	Helper
Type Three	The Achiever/Status Seeker	Performer	Succeeder
Type Four	The Individualist/Artist	Tragic Romantic	Individualist
Type Five	The Investigator/Thinker	Observer	Observer
Type Six	The Loyalist	Trooper/Devil's Advocate	Guardian
Type Seven	The Enthusiast/Generalist	Epicure	Dreamer
Type Eight	The Challenger/Leader	Boss	Confronter
Type Nine	The Peacemaker	Mediator	Preservationist

As a teaching device, the different names assigned to each type can be a helpful rhetorical method for remembering them. This can get complicated, however, because there are as many different labels for each of the nine types as there are Enneagram schools of thought. The most commonly used are borrowed from Don Riso and Russ Hudson's Enneagram Institute and Helen Palmer's Enneagram in the Narrative Tradition (I also like Kathleen Hurley and Theodore Dobson's contributions to the naming of the types).

Sometimes, easier than appealing to the names to describe the chief characteristic of the types, people find that working around a circle based on fundamental needs is a better way to self-type as well as remember the types.

I first learned the Enneagram by aligning a distinguishing need with each of the numbers. These needs emerged from the evolution of Father Richard Rohr and Andreas Ebert's groundbreaking work on the Enneagram.

In 1989 Father Richard and his coauthor published the German-language Enneagram classic *Das Enneagram: Die 9 Gesichter der Seele*. The success of the book was overwhelming and led to its first English translation in 1990, *Discovering the Enneagram: An Ancient Tool for a New Spiritual Journey*. It also established Father Richard as one of the prominent Western thought-leaders and modern Christian teachers of the Enneagram.

In the 1980s and early 1990s, the development of the Enneagram's usefulness was expanding at a feverish pace. By 2001 Father Richard and Ebert had revised and updated their original work, republishing it in its popular form today, *The Enneagram: A Christian Perspective.** From both *Discovering the Enneagram* and *The Enneagram:*

---

* Rohr and Ebert continued the conversation with a few other key Enneagram innovators and published *Erfahrungen mit dem Enneagram: Sich selbust und Gott begegnen* in 1991 with a 1992 English edition titled *Experiencing the Enneagram*.

A *Christian Perspective* I learned the nine types not by name but by these needs:

Type One	The Need to Be Perfect
Type Two	The Need to Be Needed
Type Three	The Need to Succeed
Type Four	The Need to Be Special (or Unique)
Type Five	The Need to Perceive (or Understand)
Type Six	The Need to Be Sure/Certain (or Secure)
Type Seven	The Need to Avoid Pain
Type Eight	The Need to Be Against
Type Nine	The Need to Avoid

Whether names or needs, these quick reference handles merely keep us at the surface of the possibilities of the Enneagram. Simply describing nine personality profiles or nine sets of charming imperfections and endearing habits limits us from telling ourselves the truth about what the Enneagram spotlights.

THE HOLY IDEAS AND THE VIRTUES

Another approach to understanding the nine types involves the exploration of the purest features of each type—the Enneagram's Holy Ideas and Virtues.

Much like a precious jewel, with each twist and turn reflecting the elegance of a different facet, the Enneagram also has affirmative renderings that draw attention to what is particularly beautiful about each type.

In his renderings of the Enneagram, Óscar Ichazo (the man who interpreted and brought forward the Enneagram in its modern form) proposed an Enneagram of Holy Ideas and an Enneagram of Virtues. Simply put, the Holy Idea of each type is the *mental clarity* of the True Self that emerges when the mind is at rest, while the Virtue of each type is the *emotional objectivity* of the True Self that comes forward in a heart at peace. Much like the nine Beatitudes from Matthew 5:1–12 or the nine fruit of the Spirit listed in Galatians 5:22–23, the evidence of wholeness is manifested through our peace of mind and heart revealed in our Holy Idea and Virtue. Together, our Holy Idea and Virtue express who we were always created to be.

The Holy Ideas of the Enneagram epitomize the lucidity of a mind integrated with one's heart and body, evidenced in the consolidation of mindfulness and self-realization.

The traditional Holy Ideas as developed by Ichazo are as follows:

Type One	Perfection
Type Two	Will, Freedom
Type Three	Harmony, Hope
Type Four	Origin
Type Five	Transparency
Type Six	Strength, Faith
Type Seven	Wisdom
Type Eight	Truth
Type Nine	Love

For example, when type Ones disentangle themselves from their idealized drive for perfectionism, they realize that everything is already just as it should be; as Father Richard (a type One himself) says, "Everything belongs"—the good, the bad, and the ugly. In this case, perfectionism is no longer a cruel master but a gentle guide back to grounded presence, perfect peace, *holy perfection.*

Or take the restlessness of people dominant in type Four, always longing to discover their intriguing exceptionalism. When the delusions of their ego are confronted by their True Self, they rest in the gift of their purpose for being. Centered Fours know they were created for a reason, that God is their source, and that being inseparable from the Source displays the reality of their *holy origin.*

HOLY IDEAS

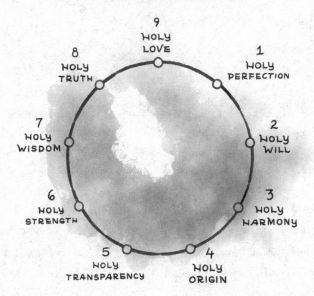

9
HOLY
LOVE

8
HOLY
TRUTH

1
HOLY
PERFECTION

7
HOLY
WISDOM

2
HOLY
WILL

6
HOLY
STRENGTH

3
HOLY
HARMONY

5
HOLY
TRANSPARENCY

4
HOLY
ORIGIN

If the Holy Ideas of the Enneagram display the fruit of a mind at peace, then the Virtues of the Enneagram draw attention to the by-products of a heart at rest, a heart that is centered and present. The Virtues of the Enneagram are the unexpected fecundity that surprises us when we are aligned with what is good, true, and beautiful within our identity. The Virtues illuminate for us the very best of what our hearts were created for, what each of us uniquely contributes to the kind of peace-filled world we all desire to live in.

The traditional Virtues of each type are as follows:

Type One	Serenity
Type Two	Humility
Type Three	Truthfulness, Authenticity
Type Four	Equanimity, Emotional Balance
Type Five	Detachment
Type Six	Courage
Type Seven	Sobriety
Type Eight	Innocence
Type Nine	Action

Returning to type One, when the mind is set at ease that God's perfection is enough, then the heart rests in *serenity*, unbothered by what seems to be imperfect. The peace-filled heart of the One is no longer driven by its inner compulsions to fix everything, but instead savors what is.

Returning to type Four, when the mind knows its origin,

identity is rooted in the Source of love. Then the *emotional balance* of their heart allows them to be present in the extremes of all their feelings—their anguish and turmoil, as well as their effervescence and exuberance, all have a place, but don't need to define or control them.

VIRTUES

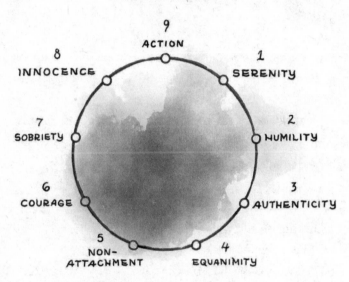

Being able to caricature nine kinds of people might be an interesting dinner party trick, but it only reinforces the reductionism of categorizing individuals, which in the end dehumanizes everyone. The Enneagram offers much more under the surface. Its various facets—the names and needs, the Holy Ideas and Virtues—give us practical handles to better identify and understand our type. By digging deeper into the *why* behind each type we start to unravel the mystery of our True Self and essential nature. This is the real substance we aim for.

WHAT ABOUT THE ENNEAGRAM SYMBOL?

By now, you may be starting to see where you fall within the nine types. To further help in this process, the Enneagram offers a handy visual aid.

The word *Enneagram* is translated from two Greek words, *ennea* meaning "nine" and *gramma* meaning a sign "drawn" or "written" (from which the word *diagram* also is derived).

At its surface, the Enneagram is drawn as a figure with nine equidistant points resting on the circumference of a circle; each of the points is connected within the circle by nine lines. Centered at the top of the circle, the top of these nine points is the tip of an equilateral triangle; the remaining six points of the diagram form an irregular hexagram symbol.

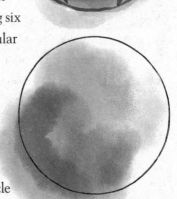

The figure itself contains significant symbolism.

First, the circle denotes eternity, unity, wholeness, and the inclusivity of all things—the *Law of One*. Without a beginning or end, the circle illustrates the everlasting essence of love—think of a wedding ring, for example. And while the Enneagram is used and studied across religions, Christians may find in its imagery an expression of the unending love of God. This notion of oneness contains all that is and was and will be.

Second, the equilateral triangle within the Enneagram's circle illustrates what is known as the *Law of Three**—the three forces that guide everything in motion: active, passive, and neutral. The tombs in which ancient Egyptians laid to rest the remains of their royalty (thought to be deities) were built as pyramids, usually in the shape of four triangles resting against each other to form a single point at the top. The ancient Greek letter Δ (*delta*) was drawn in the shape of a triangle and often used as a symbol for doorways or openings. Early Christians used the triangle as a symbol of the Trinity to help explain the three consubstantial persons of the divine nature of God. And in geometry a line extends infinitely in both directions, but a line segment has two points marking its beginning and its end; by adding a third point, a triangle is formed, symbolically elevating the polarities and adding depth to what was once one-dimensional. The three points of this equilateral triangle within the Enneagram's circle are marked with the numbers denoting types Nine, Three, and Six.

Third, the irregular, crisscrossed six-pointed hexagram within the Enneagram's circle is what is used to teach the *Law of Seven*. The Law of Seven is thought to explain the spectrums of things like light (refracted through the seven colors of a rainbow), sound (heard through

* For a further understanding of this concept from a historic Christian perspective, check out Cynthia Bourgeault's *The Holy Trinity and the Law of Three: Discovering the Radical Truth at the Heart of Christianity* (Boulder, CO: Shambhala Publications, 2016).

the seven fundamental tones of an octave), sequence (the seven days of a week forming the basic interval to measure time), and energy (the seven chakras of the body's energy centers that yoga students learn).

In Judaism and later Christianity, the origins of the entire cosmos are told through a creation narrative lasting six days with a seventh day punctuating its completion. Throughout Christian scripture the number seven is used to symbolize perfection. Even the Roman Catholic Church utilizes seven graces or sacraments as the means of eternal salvation.

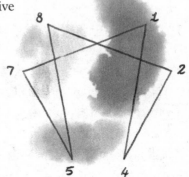

Much like the six days of creation, the Law of Seven overlaid on the Enneagram symbol consists of six points marked with the numbers One, Four, Two, Eight, Five, and Seven.*

But the Enneagram is much more than a mere symbol.

THE ANCIENT ORIGINS OF THE ENNEAGRAM

Versions of the Enneagram have been around for thousands of years, hidden away in wisdom schools and passed along orally within the

---

* The curious relationship these six points have with seven is hidden in the numbers in perpetuity behind the decimal point of the quotient of any whole number divided by seven other than seven itself. For example:

$1 \div 7 = 0.142857\ldots$
$2 \div 7 = 0.285714\ldots$
$3 \div 7 = 0.428571\ldots$
$4 \div 7 = 0.571428\ldots$
$5 \div 7 = 0.714285\ldots$
$6 \div 7 = 0.857142\ldots$

The infinite repetition of these numbers in this particular order is important because by drawing lines between the points of the Enneagram's hexagram following this pattern, the figure itself emerges. It's also curious to note that if you keep these numbers in order starting with one and multiply that number by seven, the number nine reemerges: 142,857 x 7 = 999,999.

mystic traditions of the world's religions. Its origin is highly disputed and hotly contested, the stuff of myths and legends.

In *The Sufi Enneagram* by Dr. Laleh Bakhtiar (one of the world's leading Sufi Enneagram experts), it's suggested the Enneagram may be as "old as Babylon,"[2] while others claim there is evidence the Enneagram first showed up over six thousand years ago in ancient Egypt.

I have been told of the Enneagram in prehistoric Korea as well as a version in folk Buddhism. Once after I led an Enneagram retreat in Cambodia, one of the participants commented, "We have this in Buddhism; I grew up learning about something like this through my family's tradition."

Perhaps the oldest recorded hint of the Enneagram may be in what Beatrice Chestnut speculates to be evidence hidden away in Homer's classic work, *The Odyssey*.

> One of the first written texts in [W]estern literature, *The Odyssey* tells the story of the metaphoric journey "home" to the "[T]rue [S]elf." In the story, the hero, Odysseus (the guy who thought up the "Trojan Horse"), returning home from the Trojan War, travels to nine "lands" populated with mythic creatures whose characters match the nine Enneagram types exactly—in the same order as the modern teaching![3]

A Greek contemporary of the Buddha, philosopher and mathematician Pythagoras (who coincidentally studied in Egypt) fused mysticism and mathematics and developed the Law of Three. He is said to have used a drawing resembling the Enneagram symbol as his spiritual signature after learning of it in Heliopolis, which was the center of worship of the Ennead or the nine deities of ancient Egyptian mythology.

Others point to the Jewish philosopher Philo (who also happened to live in Egypt), hinting that perhaps his esoteric Judaism and the Tree of Life, which is considered the key symbol of the tradition of the Kabbalah, root the earliest forms of the Enneagram in Jewish mysticism.

Much has been written to suggest that the early Egyptian Christian monastic ascetics, the desert mothers and fathers, were the chief architects of the Enneagram, led by the fourth-century mystic Evagrius Ponticus. Ponticus's writings are often cited to support theories on the Christian origins of the Enneagram, specifically as it relates to his work on his list of eight vices and virtues (in one place he names nine), which closely resemble the nine Virtues and Passions of the Enneagram as we have it today.[4]

Very commonly, many of today's experts credit Sufi communities spread throughout Central Asia, from Iraq to Afghanistan, for developing the Enneagram between the thirteenth and sixteenth centuries.

Regardless of whether the Enneagram has its roots in Buddhism, Judaism, Christianity, or Islam, we do know that it wasn't until the early 1900s that an Eastern Orthodox man, G. I. Gurdjieff, introduced the modern form of the Enneagram to the Western world.

A CONTESTED HISTORY OF THE ENNEAGRAM:
George Gurdjieff, Óscar Ichazo, and Claudio Naranjo

George Ivanovich Gurdjieff was born in the Russian city of Alexandropol (now Gyumri, Armenia) sometime between the late 1860s and mid 1870s. Gurdjieff grew up in the town of Kars (now in Turkey), stationed on the ancient Silk Road that for centuries connected the East and the West, the hinge between Asia and Europe. Because of its curious history and the influence of its ancient trade routes, Kars was unusually multicultural, so Gurdjieff achieved fluency in several languages at a young age. Kars also provided access to several religious traditions that Gurdjieff found so compelling that he all but abandoned his early ambitions of the priesthood to become a student of philosophy, religion, and wisdom traditions.

Gurdjieff joined Seekers of the Truth, a group "committed to the quest for hidden knowledge."[5] With fellow pilgrims, Gurdjieff spent the following decades searching for esoteric truths through which they could understand the world. His travels took him as far as Tibet and France, as well as to many places in between, including Egypt. Along the way, he uncovered rumors and fragments of a teaching that he would eventually realize was the Enneagram. While there are tales of a secret brotherhood passing along this teaching, Gurdjieff never disclosed the specifics of where he learned of the Enneagram, though it was apparent that it became one of the core sources of his teachings.

As Gurdjieff developed his understanding of the Enneagram, he was convinced that it could be used as an overlay to explain any evolved system, be it religion, science, or astrology. "*Everything* can be included and read in the Enneagram,"[6] he said.

Gurdjieff also believed the Enneagram was constantly in motion and must be taught through movement and choreography. He was considered a collector of mystical dances that he taught his disciples as a way of transmitting the wisdom of the Enneagram.

Unlike modern Enneagram teaching, Gurdjieff's study was more on a cosmic level than an individual level. Nonetheless, his teaching on the three Intelligence Centers gave his followers nuanced hints to what has now become the primary way of understanding a modern application of the Enneagram.*

---

* Of all the contemporary Enneagram teachers and schools, the Enneagram Institute has made a strong commitment to honor Gurdjieff in the way it imparts the primary aspects of the Enneagram. Its website further explains this notion of "chief feature": "The chief feature is the lynchpin of a person's ego structure—the basic characteristic that defines them. Gurdjieff generally used colorful language to describe a person's chief feature, often using the Sufi tradition of telling the person what kind of idiot they were. People could be round idiots, square idiots, subjective hopeless idiots, squirming idiots, and so forth. But Gurdjieff never taught anything about a system of understanding character related to the Enneagram symbol."

The little we know of Gurdjieff utilizing the Enneagram to describe one's *essential nature* as opposed to one's personality took place at dinner parties where wine, vodka, brandy, and Armagnac flowed generously to loosen the defense mechanisms of his guests. Over these elaborate meals, in typical type Eight fashion, not meant to be taken personally, he goaded his dinner guests by describing them as "various kinds of idiots" or "worms" based on their thinking, feeling, or physical reactions to his provocations.[7] Around the table Gurdjieff asked his guests to align themselves with the kind of person they thought they were and thus began his toasting of them as "idiots"—perhaps the first term used for *type*.[8]

Peter D. Ouspensky, one of Gurdjieff's most notable mentees, studied directly under Gurdjieff for ten years before unfortunately splitting off from his teacher. Two years after Ouspensky's death, his followers published what has become an essential account of what he learned from Gurdjieff, *In Search of the Miraculous* (Ouspensky had originally titled the work *Fragments from an Unknown Teaching*). The book, published in 1949, contains a drawing of Gurdjieff's Enneagram and states that Gurdjieff first introduced the Enneagram to his students in Moscow in 1916 at his Institute for the Harmonious Development of Man.

In 1954, just five years after Ouspensky's book was published, Óscar Ichazo, the Bolivian-born founder of the Arica wisdom school (the Quechua word for "open door"), laid claim to the modern use of the Enneagram. Ichazo developed 108 different iterations of the Enneagram which he called Enneagons, the most well-known today focusing around what are now widely accepted as the Enneagram's traditional *Passions*, *Fixations*, *Virtues*, *Holy Ideas*, *wings*, and the theory of what the lines between the numbers symbolize.

Some controversy exists around Ichazo's claim that his development of the Enneagram had no direct ties to any of Gurdjieff's writings or students, chiefly Ouspensky's essential work. Rather, Ichazo attributed his discovery of the Enneagram to his world travels, which may have included exposure to the Sarmoung Brotherhood (the same group of esoteric Sufis thought to have taught Gurdjieff the Enneagram), and to a seven-day vision in which he claims an angel visited him with the teaching of the Enneagram. In 1969–70, Ichazo passed on this teaching of the Enneagram as one way to understand human essence to the Chilean Gestalt psychologist Claudio Naranjo.

During one of their first meetings Naranjo remembers, "He [Ichazo] drew an Enneagram with the names of the Passions at the corresponding points and asked me to situate myself on the map. I suggested two hypotheses, and got it wrong both times."[9] Despite his lack of immediate success with the Enneagram, Naranjo built on Ichazo's ideas and did the most significant work to develop the *Ennea-Types* now popularly used in the modern application of the Enneagram as a psychological profiling system.

From Gurdjieff's provocations and Naranjo's own initial mistyping, we see the humanity in the modern founders of the Enneagram—men not meant to be canonized or venerated but teachers whose flawed humanity drew them deeper into the gifts of the Enneagram.

In 1970 Naranjo and Ichazo apparently had a cordial parting of ways; still, Ichazo gave Naranjo conditional permission to teach the Enneagram. Later that year, in the backyard of his home in Berkeley, California, Naranjo gathered his original Seekers After Truth group (named in honor of Gurdjieff's collective of wisdom seekers) under the condition of secrecy, and each week for nearly four years transmitted the Enneagram of Personality. That first little group of fifteen to twenty participants included an art student, barely twenty-one years old, Sandra Maitri, who since has published essential works on the spiritual dimensions of the Enneagram. Another notable student in that original group was a graduate student at

UC Berkeley, A. Hameed Ali (A. H. Almaas), who developed the Diamond Approach to Self-Realization.

Sandra Maitri remembers, "Naranjo's approach was to integrate psychological and spiritual work, which at the time was a remarkable innovation. It was out of this ground that we worked with the Enneagram."[10] Naranjo developed the now common use of the Enneagram in Western psychology; his teaching helped establish the Enneagram as a character-structure tool for typing people based on nine common human archetypes.

Made explicit through signed confidentiality commitments, Naranjo insisted that none of his students write or teach about the Enneagram until he had granted them permission. However, a young Jesuit, Robert Ochs, took his hand-scribbled notes from listening to Naranjo and, excited about what he was learning, began passing along his newly acquired wisdom to twelve members of his community at Loyola University in Chicago. Ochs even made those he shared it with promise not to teach it for two years until they had integrated into their own lives the meaning of the Enneagram. But many of the young Jesuits couldn't resist sharing their revelations, and soon the Enneagram was let loose into the wild.

The first Enneagram book published in the West came out in 1984, and since then the Enneagram has continued to grow in popularity, gaining momentum through accessibility. Some of the early innovators of the Enneagram whose books appealed broadly include Don Riso (coauthor with Russ Hudson of *The Wisdom of the Enneagram*), who as a seminarian in Toronto learned it through his Jesuit connections to Ochs; and Helen Palmer, who studied with Naranjo in the early 1970s.

From its ancient roots to its modern application, the practical utility of the Enneagram has been appropriated by the CIA to profile world leaders, written about in *The Paris Review, Newsweek, Forbes,* and CNN.com, and taught in graduate courses at several academic institutions, including Stanford University. The Enneagram is even used to explain leadership styles and decision making styles in the workplace.

What is unfortunate is the series of broken ties starting with Gurdjieff and Ouspensky, then between Ichazo and Naranjo, and then between Naranjo and those of his students who broke their confidentiality contract. Today there is an urgent need to heal the divide among those who assert *their* explanation of the Enneagram as the only authentic way of teaching it. It's hard to take such assertions seriously since the Enneagram of Personality is clearly a modern invention in its infancy.

Given that the Enneagram is a system that may have thousands of years of hidden history yet has only fifty to sixty years of application in its modern form, now is an exciting time to explore the possibilities of what is still to be uncovered. It's no overstatement to suggest that we hardly understand what we are working with, so we would do well to take a learning stance of humility. This begins with recognizing that the Enneagram can't be reduced to a personality test and that we have much more to learn. As Russ Hudson frequently emphasizes, "*Type* isn't a 'type' of person, but a path to God."

The nine types of the Enneagram form a sort of *color wheel* that describes the basic archetypes of humanity's tragic flaws, sin tendencies, primary fears, and unconscious needs. The understanding of these components, when shaped through contemplative practice, helps us wake up to our True Self and come home to our essential nature.

As a sacred map to our soul, the Enneagram is a blueprint for developing character that each of us carries throughout our life, but one that we don't open until we discover our type.

Now I would be remiss not to mention that some individuals have concerns about the contested origins of the Enneagram, especially when viewed from a Christian perspective. I'm frequently asked if the Enneagram is a New Age teaching or has roots in the occult. Others want to know where the Enneagram shows up in the Bible. I can understand the apprehension; I myself wasn't too sure about the Enneagram when I first learned about it.

I was raised to be suspicious of anything that could possibly misalign with Christianity. I grew up in a youth group that tried to convince me secular music was evil (allegedly, a lot of Satanic messages were backward-masked into popular music in the 1980s). The Christian university I attended didn't allow students to dance or drink alcohol—in fact, we also couldn't have tattoos or piercings or wear shorts on campus until after 5:00 p.m. During my childhood, my parents wouldn't even let my siblings and me watch *The Smurfs*, *Scooby-Doo*, *Gremlins*, or *Ghostbusters* (though the Narnia stories, the Lord of the Rings trilogy, and the Star Wars movies were somehow street-legal). Oh yeah, and Halloween was for sure off limits.

Much of that seems pretty trivial now (and my parents got past some of those old hang-ups, and it turns out, of course, they're pretty cool). But I do understand and respect the questions used to discern what faithful living looks like in the world today.

In regard to the Enneagram, you may have some questions yourself. I've found it helpful to affirm that as the origin of truth itself, Divine Love is in all truth no matter where it may be found. This is where discernment is critical for women and men on their own faith journeys.

From personal experience, I can tell you with confidence that the Enneagram has been one of the most important aids in my spiritual formation, and many other people I know would attest to that as well. Its role in bringing about a transformed life bears out its holy validity. And thanks in large part to the great work done by Father Richard and others to bring a Christian perspective to this ancient tool, evangelical seminaries and churches everywhere are incorporating the Enneagram into their curriculum. But if it's weirding you out a bit, that's okay; the Enneagram might not be for you, or this might not be the right time in your life to dig into it. In my experience, it seems like it always shows up right on time.

The Enneagram and its origins have a storied history, to be sure. But it is also a time-tested universal theory of human nature that stands to offer us treasured insights about ourselves: why we do what we do, what God created us for, and how to bridge the gap between.

NATURE OR NURTURE?

So where does our Enneagram type come from? How is it formed within us?

The Enneagram's nine ways or nine types describe the raw material of humanity's integral fears and desires. It's widely agreed upon that every one of us possesses bits of all nine types, but a dominant type emerges in each of us. What's less widely agreed upon is *how* type comes to be part of our human experience. Is Enneagram type a product of nurture or nature?

Some believe that our first experiences of being human, coupled with adversity, suffering, or trauma, form mental and emotional rails, so to speak. Our ego then sets the train car (our personality) on these rails. Notions of the Enneagram's Original Wounds* or Childhood Wounds help support this theory, but the word *wound* in this instance can be misleading. For example, do primary caregivers really wound their firstborn by bringing another child into the family? Surely a

---

* I find Kathleen Hurley and Theodore Dobson's term "Original Wound" a more accurate portrayal of the original shock our three levels of consciousness absorb than the term "Childhood Wound" because of the assumption that Childhood Wounds were caused by or inflicted upon us by our caregiver(s).

young, tender ego may find the loss of attention to be a wound (or at least the loss of being the sole center of attention), but these sorts of early childhood experiences are common enough and, when assessed, don't create predictable personality structures.

One would imagine that if our dominant type were largely the fruit of our environment and nurturing, then parenting formulas could force or produce Enneagram types in children. But as any parent knows, it's nearly impossible to control personality through parenting techniques.

Though I understand the intention around using the language of Childhood Wounds, it's important to be clear about what we mean when appealing to the term. Perhaps the Enneagram's Childhood Wound might be better framed as the way we absorb the burden of our caregiver(s) transferring their shadow.

As children, we internalized the pain of imperfect upbringings because we didn't have the psychological capacity to process the impression of our caregiver's shadow which develops when we let our pain go unprocessed and unresolved. Our shadow—and we all have one—is the part of our ego we are unable to consciously recognize. Though it is neither good nor bad, it is where we unconsciously "park" some of the worst of ourselves—destructive patterns, addictions, or other seemingly unpresentable parts.

This internalization of pain isn't a real wound per se but a result of transmitting and absorbing our human inability to love perfectly as well as receive love perfectly.

This doesn't mean our caregivers get a pass for the mistakes they made, but it does take the blame off them. There are real physical and emotional wounds we experience as children, but the Enneagram's Childhood Wound idea is better understood as an attack on our original innocence or our original Virtue, not necessarily a physical or emotional trauma (though both could be true). And so I sometimes opt to use "attack on Virtue" as a clearer term for what is traditionally meant by "Childhood Wound." This term helps explain the Childhood Wound of the Enneagram as a loss of contact with our True Self or a loss of contact with presence.

For more than twenty years, my wife Phileena and I directed an international organization focused on meeting the needs of vulnerable children living in severely under-resourced communities. Our work included helping set up children's homes, drop-in centers for extremely poor and vulnerable youth, care facilities for children impacted by the global AIDS pandemic, and small business initiatives for young women who had been trafficked into the commercial sex industry. Most of the children and youth we worked among had experienced unspeakable harm and abuse in the forms of violence, sexual exploitation, loss of family, and loss of home—*real* childhood wounds, in many cases intentionally perpetrated against them. If personality structure is predictable, then these kids should have proved the case that Enneagram type is directly correlated to nurture and that actual wounds form or fortify type. But there was little to no direct correlation between the trauma they had experienced and the Enneagram types they reflected.

Even among the experts, the descriptions of the Childhood Wounds or the nine attacks on the nine Virtues are hotly debated. I find the consensus about the different descriptions generally accurate, but it is important to remember these are more or less (over) simplifications rather than clinically diagnosed pathologies. In fact, it's common for people to agree a version of these descriptions feels familiar from their childhood, and it's important to validate a person's sense of what may have caused their own disconnect from their original Virtue.

In my opinion, the best resource for locating basic descriptions of each of the nine attacks on our Enneagram Virtues is the *EnneaApp* created by Elan BenAmi, MA, LPC, with material provided by Lori Ohlson, MA, LPC. This list may be the clearest, but it may simply explain impressions rather than actual experiences.

Type One: These children felt heavily criticized, punished, or not good enough. Household rules may have felt inconsistent. As such, they became obsessed with being good or not making mistakes to avoid condemnation. The principal message was "You always must be better than you are."

Type Two: These children felt loved only if they were helping or pleasing others; their personal needs felt selfish. As a result, they closed off their own needs and feelings and turned to those of others. Love became defined as giving to others—though the love often didn't feel received or reciprocated.

Type Three: These children felt rewarded only for what they did and how well they did it. Their feelings were discounted and ignored; only their performance and what was expected of them mattered. This harmed their ability to love themselves and others. Admiration replaced real love.

Type Four: These children felt abandoned by one or both caretakers. They felt alone, cut off from the source of love for reasons they couldn't understand. They were not "seen" or mirrored, and felt different from their parents. As a result, they turned inward to their feelings and imagination to cope in isolation.

Type Five: These children received no meaningful interaction, emotion, or affection from caretakers. Or they had intrusive, overcontrolling parent(s) and felt exposed and defenseless in the face of this intrusion. As a result, they built walls around themselves and retreated to the mental realm.

Type Six: These children were raised in an unpredictable situation with no safe place to go. They lost faith they would ever be protected. As such, they turned to their own inner defense of doubting—disbelieving reality and rejecting their own instincts and inner guidance.

Type Seven: These children were deprived of nurturing, or it was too soon removed. They handled this lack by searching for distractions to minimize or repress the fear and pain. They decided to focus on positive options and rely on themselves to fulfill their desires and gain a sense of nurturance.

Type Eight: These children often grew up in an unsafe environment (emotionally and/or physically) and had to mature way too soon. They didn't feel safe to show any vulnerability and may have felt controlled. Weakness was used against them, so they focused only on building their strength.

Type Nine: These children were overlooked or neglected and felt unimportant or "lost." They were ignored or attacked for having needs or expressing themselves (especially anger) and decided to keep a low profile and instead focus on the needs and experiences of others.

These descriptions of what prompts our loss of contact with our True Self should birth in us a deep compassion for our own selves as well as others. If we understand these experiences as our caregivers' inability to love perfectly and the ways we absorbed that, we are more capable of viewing these pains as invitations for inner growth and healing.

I'm reminded of the story in John 9:1–3:

> As Jesus walked along, he saw someone who had been blind from birth. The disciples asked Jesus, "Rabbi, was it this individual's sin that caused the blindness, or that of the parents?" "Neither," answered Jesus. "It wasn't because of anyone's sin—not this person's, nor the parents'. Rather, it was to let God's works shine forth in this person."

It's curious that Jesus' companions wanted to place blame on someone for the person's disability. I imagine if we hold on to the language of Childhood Wound here, we also will find ways of attributing blame to our caregiver(s) for many of our own personal limitations.

But Jesus acknowledges the blindness wasn't the fault of anyone, but rather an opportunity for God's restoration to be made manifest.

The story continues in John 9:6–7:

Jesus spat on the ground, made mud with his saliva and smeared the blind one's eyes with the mud. Then Jesus said, "Go, wash in the pool of Siloam." So the person went off to wash, and came back able to see.

This story helps us answer the question, are we suffering the pathology of how we were hurt or neglected in our childhood? Is it because someone harmed us or is it because we actually *need* an obvious limitation as an invitation to give ourselves to our inner work?

The symbols here are loaded with significance. Jesus heals the person's blindness by rubbing mud (the raw material of our humanity, getting back to where we came from and where we're ultimately headed) in his eyes sockets and then instructing him to go wash in the water.

This is what the Enneagram shows us: that in returning to the literal organic matter of our humanity (the soil that echoes, "From dust we came and to dust we shall return") we come to terms with not only our limitations but the miraculous potential of that which we uncover.

Washing the mud out of our eyes is a subtle metaphor for baptism, a second form of birth that cleanses the harm from our childhood while also inviting us to return to what wounded us as children so that our eyes may be opened to the gift of who we are and who we can become.

This biblical account helps shed light on the mystery of type and shows how the very effects and limitations of our Childhood Wound are invitations to wholeness, not tragic flaws that can't be overcome.

While some Enneagram experts argue that type is essentially formed by nurture, others suggest we are born with an affinity toward a dominant type and predisposed to that type regardless of our earliest childhood impressions. I'd argue that this theory finds support in sets of twins who grew up in the same (or similar in some cases) home, in the same environment, with the same caregiver(s), and with the same access to opportunity and resources, but in their adult lives clearly identify with different Enneagram types.

My first Enneagram teacher and mentor, Father Richard, has suggested that Enneagram type is one-third nature, one-third nurture, and one-third the decision we make as children to fill a role needed to survive or thrive in our families and environments.

I personally believe we are born into our type and there's nothing our environment can do to change that. Rather, every experience we translate through our type consolidates its impression on us. It's as if when we're born, our soul lands on an arbitrary place on the circle of the Enneagram, and from that perspective of the world we develop attitudes we embrace as a way of framing context for every experience we'll ever have.

This theory suggests then that the Childhood Wound doesn't actually form type in people but is absorbed as a form of *confirmation bias,* or used to validate the affinity toward a dominant type that is gifted to us at birth.

Another common question frequently raised is *when* does our type take hold? Again, conflicting positions have yet to congeal around an accepted consensus.

Many of the great teachers caution people to steer clear of the Enneagram until they've entered their late twenties or early thirties. But my sense is that in the evolution of our human consciousness, we are more capable of recognizing our dominant type at earlier ages—especially if we have experienced great love or loss, great pain or joy, or have given ourselves to developing a rich inner life through spiritual practice and contemplative prayer—mindful ways of nurturing our spirituality that are framed by solitude, silence, and stillness.

However, I frequently find myself cautioning parents who think they've been able to type their children, sometimes even before the children could speak. Coming to terms with our type is a rite of passage, a sacred experience that should be owned by each of us when we are ready for it. Additionally, for the first few decades of life, we're still coming into our own sense of self, stretching the limits of our personalities and psyches. Having the freedom to do that without our type being assumed for us by a caregiver allows necessary personal development to remain unhindered.

In some cases I have seen young adults come to terms with their type after having been typed differently by a caregiver. Sometimes the impact of the mistyping can be devastating, causing enormous pain and profound confusion. Parents do better to *focus on their own type* and how it affects their parenting commitments rather than typing (or mistyping) their children—a mistake that could have agonizing consequences.

Resisting the impulse to attempt to type others, especially our children, allows for the mystery of type to emerge apart from other aspects of one's personality. This is helpful because, without understanding the "why" behind type, we sometimes mistake personality or temperament for essence, which only keeps our type hidden from us.

Temperament is an aspect of type, but it's just one fragment that makes up the whole of who we are. For example, some of us draw energy from being around other people, which is frequently noted as a mark of an extroverted temperament, while others who acquire inner energy from being alone are assumed to be more introverted. While attitudes and moods fluctuate, our temperament is a disposition that nonetheless may change as we mature. It's not uncommon for extremely extroverted people to move toward introversion later in life. Temperament is also exposed in people who tend to be naturally optimistic while others are pessimistic. But optimism and pessimism often fluctuate depending on our frame of mind, the kind of company we keep, or the phases of life we cycle through.

Unlike temperament, our dominant Enneagram type stays with us throughout our lives; *type does not change.* I like to think of the various results of the profile tools and tests we appeal to in an effort to learn about ourselves as the egoic *spaces we inhabit.*

One way to illustrate this is to view our temperament (often categorized as one of sixteen combinations of basic preferences that can be determined through the MBTI® inventory—a typology developed by Isabel Briggs Myers and her mother Katharine Briggs based on Carl Jung's typology theory) as the specific *room we stay in*; our StrengthsFinder® results (based on Gallup University's list of thirty-four talent themes, a weighted list of innate strengths that carry potential to increase a person's performance success) as the *way we decorate our room*; but our Enneagram type as the *kind of home we build* (maybe some of us live in a hip urban condo, others prefer a gable-roofed Thai-inspired house, while others are happy to call home a one-story ranch). Our Enneagram type is the home we are likely born in and will most definitely die in.

But let's not get too fatalistic about the Enneagram. It's not static like most popular profile systems; rather, it's dynamic and constantly in motion, just like our personal patterns of progress and regress. The Enneagram's movement hinges on the directions our type takes based on every choice we make, every action we take, every thought we have—all of these contribute either to our overall health, which brings about movement toward integration, or to a disordered state of unhealth, which causes movement toward disintegration.

HOW DO I DETERMINE MY TYPE?

Once you learn about the Enneagram, how do you determine your type?

There are three basic approaches to discerning type, but before mentioning those I want to emphasize that our type is *ours* to bring forward. Because the shaping of our type is partially confirmed to us though the experience of our Original or Childhood Wound, learning about our type can be painful to our memories and humiliating to our ego.

So it's worse than a "party foul" to type someone; it is an intrusion or an overreach. It's also an indication that someone doesn't understand the power and potential of the Enneagram. Moving beyond a caricature of personality traits to understand the essence behind type unearths the true offering of the Enneagram: access to incredible transformation. Until someone is ready for that, their thin understanding of the Enneagram can lead to more harm than good.

So please be careful not to "out" someone's type, even if you believe you're helping someone you think has mistyped; their type is really theirs to discover and theirs to share when they feel ready to do so.

Online Tests

When attempting to determine your type, the most popular approach is taking one of numerous Enneagram tests. Many free Enneagram tests are available online, and most of them are a suitable start to exploring what your type might be. However, if an online test is your preferred method of typing, I'd suggest paying for the Enneagram Institute's RHETI test because it is widely regarded as the most accurate, thorough, and time-tested.

Though online Enneagram tests are readily accessible, some experts advise against them for a variety of reasons, including racial, national, ethnic, or cultural biases* built into the assumptions of the questions contained within a test.

Another caution is our human tendency to "test" the test, to try to force an outcome by answering questions based on hoped-for results. If you approach an Enneagram test in this manner you will not get an accurate analysis.

Finally, another common caution is that a lack of self-awareness could lead you to answer questions based on who you wish you were, who you want to be, or even how you think other people see you.

If you do end up taking an online Enneagram test, you may find that the way the results are compiled is confusing. At nearly every workshop I teach, I hear someone suggest they are a "Seven with a Four wing" or a "Two with a Nine wing" (both impossible, as these types do not live next to each other on the circle, and both lead to confusion, not clarity, about type). Many of the online tests produce outcomes that require the testee to appeal to a professional to translate the results, which sometimes requires additional financial commitment. I generally advise people to consider only their top result when reviewing the results of their tests. If the primary type isn't accurate, then try another test or another method of determining your type.

Meet with a Trained Professional

A second approach to determining your type is meeting with someone trained in conducting typing process interviews. Enneagram

---

* An often under-interrogated but urgent invitation for the Western Enneagram community lies in the obvious and lamentable lack of ethnic diversity among its leading experts. Though the modern use of the Enneagram was codified and propagated by Óscar Ichazo and Claudio Naranjo (both South Americans), the Enneagram has since been disseminated largely through white, North American teachers. This observation has led to fierce critique of white, Western privilege and racial bias assumed to be fused into the way the Enneagram is currently taught and utilized. On the rise, however, are remarkable Enneagram authorities such as Nina Barnes, Rev. Nhien Vuong, Danielle Fanfair, Henna Minhas Garg, Talía Guerrero Gonzalez, Avon Manney, and Priabpran Punyabukkana (of PRANA Consulting in Thailand), who are decolonizing some of the cultural bias overlaid on much of the contemporary Western Enneagram material.

in the Narrative Tradition offers an excellent typing process train-ing that produces capable conversation partners who have been equipped with the skills to guide an interviewee through a series of questions that allows them to bring forward their own type through self-reflection and self-discovery.*

A typing interview can last up to an hour and may require pay-ment to the professional conducting the interview. A typing interview is particularly beneficial if you are stuck between two types and can't figure out which is your dominant type. In an interview format, the professional helps an interviewee navigate through common mistyping pairs for clarity and type discernment.†

Do Your Own Research

Finally, most experts agree that if you are honest with yourself and courageous enough to explore the borderlands of your own psy-che, then merely reading the thick descriptions of each of the nine types will be a sufficient method for determining your type. As you read through the materials, the type you feel most exposed by or most uncomfortable with is usually the one that ends up being yours. Doing your own research requires a level of maturity that assumes self-awareness and truthfulness. Because these assumptions are critical to an accurate self-typing process, many of the Enneagram's experts have cautioned people against exploring the Enneagram until they've reached their thirties.

Personally, I don't think age needs to be a determining factor in

---

* The Enneagram in the Narrative Tradition also trains and certifies teachers who conduct interactive panel interviews during which participants are taken through a sophis-ticated inquiry process that allows them to bring their own type forward. Though a powerful method to help a person discover their type, Enneagram panels can also be confusing when participants who have unknowingly mistyped attempt to represent a type other than their own—which demonstrates another reason why professionally trained Enneagram teachers are in urgent demand.

† Please check out appendix 2 for another helpful tool to find clarity regarding common mistyped pairs.

this process. As noted earlier, we've seen rapid evolution in human consciousness, and people are experiencing their "middle passage" (the Jungian term for what is often colloquially referred to as a "midlife crisis") earlier and more frequently than in past generations. As people come into a deeper awareness of self at younger ages, or bump around the bottom of life making tragic and painful mistakes earlier in life, they seem to be capable of discerning their type at younger ages as well.

Regardless of how you find your type, your personal discovery of your own type is the key to opening the sacred map of the Enneagram and beginning your journey home.

THE THEORY OF THE ENNEAGRAM'S WINGS

Like a color wheel that displays the blending of hues and shades around a vibrant circle, the Enneagram illustrates how each type mingles and mixes with the numbers on either side of it.

Most Enneagram experts agree that we can balance our type with its *wings*, or the numbers on each side of it. For example, if you are dominant in type Six, you may find yourself leaning into some of the characteristics of type Five and/or type Seven. Theories on the wings differ; some think we develop only one wing while others believe we can develop both or sit loosely between them. Father Richard suggests that as we mature, our wings may become more prominent and our dominant type less socially visible.

While we may observe that at different phases in life we're more dependent on one wing than the other, the dynamic possibilities of countless differences within type are partially rooted in our movement between and toward our wings.

I've found this true in my own life. Personally, as someone dominant in type Eight with a very strong Seven wing (signaled by playful energy), I have had to learn how to lean into my Nine wing (characterized by cooperation) to find ways of bringing diverse conversation partners together around difficult conversations or intense work environments. This of course is necessary for all Eights, who often come across as offensive or abrasive, combative or shocking; to understand how the energy of Eights can impact people requires the hard work of developing the Nine wing as a bridge for others to feel safe with them.

As always with the Enneagram, a heightened awareness of our type and tendencies can propel us into growth.

Paths *of* Integration, Disintegration, *and* Grace for the Journey

*Honestly and Compassionately Confronting
Our Patterns in Growth and Stress*

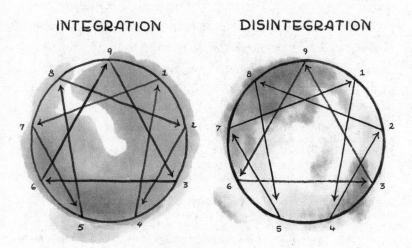

INTEGRATION   DISINTEGRATION

One fundamental component of understanding type involves the lines within the Enneagram's symbol. These crisscrossing lines show us the movement of our type when operating in a healthy or unhealthy state.*

---

* In many Enneagram books and workshops, the notion of types in their healthy and unhealthy variations is often ambiguous at best, if not entirely arbitrary. The Enneagram

There are several schools of thought about the traversing of lines inside the Enneagram, each with diverging philosophies regarding their implications. For instance, the Enneagram Institute refers to the lines as the *directions of integration* and *disintegration*; the Enneagram in the Narrative Tradition refers to them as our *Security Types* and *Stress Types*; the Chilean grandfather of the modern Enneagram, Claudio Naranjo, used the language *Heart Points* and *Stress Points*; and H. A. Almaas originated the notion of the *Soul Child*, which Father Richard and Sandra Maitri continued to develop.*

These are all different ways of describing the dynamic of each type as it presses into growth or reverts to patterns of self-sabotage. This is where we encounter the uniqueness of the Enneagram as a character-structure construct: it offers both a portrait of health and a portrait of unhealth for each type, and prompts us to identify honestly where we are functioning on that spectrum. This might vary from day to day or even hour to hour, but the gift presented to us is greater awareness that leads to psychological and spiritual growth.

Institute, however, has developed thorough descriptions of each type on a nine-rung ladder of psycho-spiritual health based specifically on a person's relationship with their Enneagram type's Basic Fear. When someone believes a malformed version of their type's Basic Fear, it is as if they take a step down this ladder, recasting a simultaneously diminished Basic Desire. The first three rungs of this ladder and their corresponding Basic Fear and Basic Desire are all considered "healthy," the next three levels are considered "average," and the bottom three levels are considered "unhealthy." The precision and clarity of the Enneagram Institute's rendering of the health of each type is worthy of consideration and should be required reading for anyone teaching or writing about the perceived "health" or "unhealth" of Enneagram types.

* Almaas, Maitri, and Rohr have suggested that perhaps our True Self or essential nature (specifically in this case, the type we were born as) is actually not the type we identify with in our adult lives but the *Heart Point* or *Security Type* of our dominant type. In this theory, the introduction of our Childhood Wound thrust us across the path of disintegration and so our lives are spent yearning for that inner child to be safe again (in other words, hoping for integration)—thus the notion of a *Soul Child*. For example, the Soul Child of type Three is type Six; in this theory, persons dominant in type Three were actually born as Sixes and are forever yearning to reconnect with that type. Following this line of thinking, our Heart Point or Security Type isn't what we integrate to but what we come home to—the fundamental essence of the deeply embedded sense of self we've somehow lost along the way. Maybe a clearer way of saying this is that our Heart Point is not a path of integration but more a realization of what we really were when born into our essential nature. To return to our *Soul Child* is a way of coming home.

The theory of what these lines between the numbers symbolize in *integration* or *security* allows our dominant type to borrow the positive traits of another type.

For example, a healthy person dominant in type One integrates or borrows some of the positive traits of type Seven by relaxing their inner drive for perfection and allowing themselves to become a little playful and spontaneous.

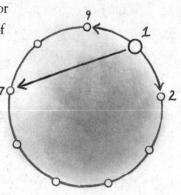

INTEGRATION

Alternatively, it looks like self-confident, healthy self-assertion when people dominate in type Two integrate, taking on the favorable features of self-expression common in type Four.

Sometimes (especially in the case of those dominant in type Three, because Threes want to accomplish self-perfection as a way to maintain an inner sense of value) people will try to intentionally develop or force movement toward integration, but my sense is that true integration is an act of pure grace, an indicator of inner health and centeredness.

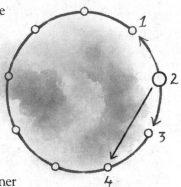

INTEGRATION

In fact, I believe that when we spend time trying to move toward integration, we are not focusing on the real inner work of facing our dominant type. So while it is helpful to see the full picture of the type we borrow from in health, the key for all of us is to focus on health and growth in our dominant type.

When we integrate, it should surprise us. It should be an unexpected reward for doing what is nourishing for our soul—and that wonderful shock of observing the gifts of our integration is the validation of the astonishing grace it is.

It is important to note that we do not *become* the type we integrate toward; it is only as we become a healthy, centered version of our dominant type that we are simultaneously able to reach across the Enneagram and essentially "borrow" positive traits. So when someone says, for example, "As a Seven, when I integrate I move to Five," that statement is only partially accurate, because the movement isn't truly *away* from one's dominant type.

There is sometimes a bit of misunderstanding that as we become healthy we move from our dominant type into our Heart Point, but we must remember that there are beautiful aspects of every type when we are at our best. To recognize ourselves in integration requires that we accept the best of ourselves *in* our dominant type.

The converse path is not exactly an inverse pattern either, so those who suggest that *disintegration* is merely borrowing the negative traits of the type on our path of disintegration are somewhat mistaken. This view also promotes a sense of self-condemnation when we're not getting it "right," but I believe there is much more grace for us here than we might first think.

Remember when as a kid you tried climbing a tree for the first time? Some of us weren't as successful as others. I remember a few classmates with plaster casts on their arms that we'd cover in graffiti with pithy bits of obnoxious advice or signatures scrawled with colorful markers. More often than not, those plaster casts were holding together the mending bones fractured by tree-climbing accidents. The lucky ones among us might have slipped off a branch but somehow appealed to a subconscious self-preservation instinct to immediately reach out and grab a tree limb on our way down.

A newer theory that I happen to agree with is that our path of disintegration is that *innate self-survival reflex* that stops our fall by reaching out to the lower-level manipulation techniques of another type as a way of getting our attention—letting us know we are falling and if we don't catch ourselves we'll "break our arm" or worse.

The path of disintegration can be understood as a subconscious self-preservation instinct to prevent an unhealthy person from falling farther down the hole they feel stuck in. For example, an anxious or fearful person dominant in type Four may start to take on the passive-aggressive manipulative techniques typical of someone dominant in type Two. This may look like a Four crossing emotional boundaries or smothering someone with too much affection. Fours disintegrate in this way as an unconscious attempt to draw people back to themselves, offering the possibility that they will be seen and validated.

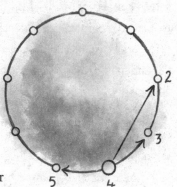

DISINTEGRATION

One of the more surprising examples of types in disintegration is that of type Five. Normally clear-headed and cerebral, people who are dominant in type Five may lose their way and fall hard into the addictive tendencies of type Seven as a way of manipulating their own inability to find answers to the problems for which they desperately need solutions.

One of the clearest tales of type Five in disintegration is Seth Haines's book, *Coming Clean: A Story of Faith*, the heart-wrenching memoir of a young man whose child is facing dire health risks and likely death. Seth knows what to do: he finds the best doctors, has his faith community say all the right prayers, and commits to being a loving and present father as he cares for his son. But nothing works.

The doctors can't help. The prayers go unanswered. His love isn't enough to protect his son from the pain.

And so he wades into the murky waters of alcoholism as his sister smuggles bottles of gin into the hospital. The constant buzz of the booze is Seth's way of dulling the constant mental activity his mind is addicted to—the continual churning and turning over of the problem in pursuit of solutions. In his own disintegration, Seth adopts type Seven's propensity to overuse or overdo anything that offers pleasure as a way of rescuing himself from mental and emotional agony.

Thankfully, his son recovered, and when Seth caught himself "falling down the tree," his own recovery began. His community came around him and he found his way back home to his better self. It wasn't easy; it never is for any of us. Being honest with ourselves can be painful—humiliating, in fact. Recognizing that dependency on alcohol can never be a substitute for dependency on God is what brought Seth clarity. His example shows each of us a simple lesson that is available to everyone in disintegration: If we can't self-observe, then we can't self-correct.

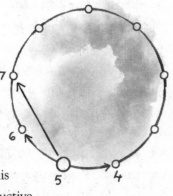

DISINTEGRATION

Surely our *path of disintegration* is an indication that we are unwell, but recognizing when we are moving in this direction helps us wake up to the destructive tendencies that keep us at our lower levels of mental and emotional health. Think of it as a warning sign or flare signal, designed not to condemn a person but to guide them back home.

Being able to recognize when we're moving in a disintegrative direction implies we have already given ourselves to the hard inner work of learning to observe our patterns, even when we're not doing well. Because when we're falling, the last thing we're usually capable of is noticing the fall. That inner work is ultimately what keeps guiding us home to our True Self.

IDENTIFYING OUR "SIN TENDENCIES" VERSUS EMBRACING IMPERFECTIONS

When I was young, my parents bought me a red plastic contraption that I would stuff full of play dough. Then, when I couldn't get any more play dough inside, I would force it out by pushing down on a long yellow lever that pressed the colorful soft clay into shapes—circles and stars and diamonds. Another way of looking at the Enneagram is just like that: if you believe in the doctrine of original sin, then the Enneagram exposes the shape of your tragic flaw—the aspect of you that is most vulnerable to sin—as it is forced from your soul through the pressure of guilt, shame, stress, anxiety, fear, frustration, or anger.

This isn't to suggest that the Enneagram only highlights the harmful ways we act out, but it does show us a pattern in the shape of the unique loop of our type that keeps us stuck. This loop has always been with us, the circular pull to reconnect with our original goodness that gets knocked off course by our original sin. This self-perpetuating loop of enduring our disconnect from the essence of our True Self can lead to addictions, and of course in addiction the environment for sin exists. Let's take a closer look at what this destructive loop looks like.

THE FIXATIONS AND PASSIONS OF THE ENNEAGRAM

Before introducing the Fixations and Passions of the Enneagram, perhaps the most well-known aspects of each type's structure, let's briefly return to the Holy Ideas and Virtues for context.

If you believe that in the earliest days of infancy we are as close to perfect as we'll ever be in our lives—the most unencumbered from our tragic flaw and the most uncontaminated by its consequences—then the Holy Ideas and Virtues of the Enneagram types are the two fundamental aspects of our soul's essence that reveal in us the raw material of our True Self.

These two features show us the original righteousness of hearts (Virtues) and minds (Holy Ideas) fully at rest in their essence.

Genesis 1:27 reads, "Humankind was created as God's reflection: in the divine image God created them; female and male, God made them." And Genesis 1:31 concludes, "God looked at all of this creation, and proclaimed that this was good—*very good*" (emphasis mine). This proclamation was made *before* Eve and Adam were sent out of Eden. Still, humanity, *very good*? Seriously?

If you grew up believing in original sin, you've probably had a hard time seeing anything "very good" in your own humanity. But the Enneagram's Holy Ideas and Virtues may actually point to what was *very good* at the beginning of creation—our best and purest sense of self before sin gummed things up.

The American Protestant theologian Reinhold Niebuhr popularized this doctrine as "original righteousness"—not just innocence, but faithfulness in relationship to God. The experience of sin then marred humanity's original righteousness.

In the incarnation, when God became human, the notion that there is goodness in humanity was restored. And with the possibility of restoration came hope for redemption. We see this when Jesus submitted himself to the sacrament of baptism (John 1:29–34), not just to locate his identity in a broader community of faith but also to reveal original righteousness for all of us: "We must do this to completely fulfill God's justice," or "righteousness," as it's translated in many other versions (Matthew 3:15).

Our Holy Idea and our Virtue, rooted in our original righteousness, spotlight our indispensable purpose for being.

It is the loss of our original righteousness, that Edenic state of sinless perfection and unbroken relationship with the Source of love, that creates the delusions of our Holy Idea and Virtue.

In the structure of each Enneagram type, the shadow of the Holy Idea is the type's traditional Fixation—*how the mind copes with the True Self's loss of perfection and presence.*

The shadow of the Virtue is the type's Passion—*how the heart aches and longs to reconnect with the Virtue of the True Self.*

The Enneagram's Fixations, the nine type-specific mental tactics used to convince an uncentered mind that its Passion is legitimate, are the inverse of the Enneagram's Holy Ideas. And the Enneagram's Passions, the nine type-specific coping skills related to each type's state of emotional imbalance, are the inverse of the Enneagram's Virtues.

	Mind/Head Center	Heart/Feeling Center
Centered	Holy Idea = Mental Clarity	Virtue = Emotional Objectivity
Uncentered	Fixation = Mental Hyperactivity	Passion = Emotional Reactivity

At the root of nearly every decision we make in life is the desire to find our way home, back to our essential nature, our True Self, and back to God. Sadly, the reality of living in the broken world outside of Eden is that we often go about this in all the wrong ways. So the Fixation and Passion of each Enneagram type become a sort of addiction loop, a misguided attempt to find our way home, back to our True Self where we are aligned with our Holy Idea and Virtue.

I think of the Fixation and Passion as a tiny flashlight that our ego attempts to use to find our way home in the dark. These are the most primitive of all our coping skills, and when we rely on them they become self-destructive patterns that ironically keep us in the dark.

The traditional Fixations of the Enneagram are as follows:

FIXATIONS

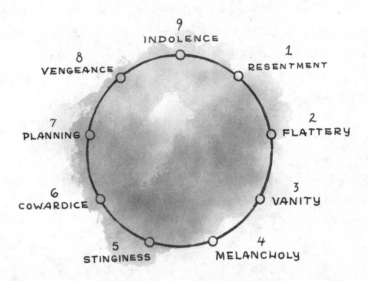

Type One	Resentment
Type Two	Flattery
Type Three	Vanity
Type Four	Melancholy
Type Five	Stinginess
Type Six	Cowardice
Type Seven	Planning
Type Eight	Vengeance
Type Nine	Indolence

The traditional Passions of the Enneagram are as follows:

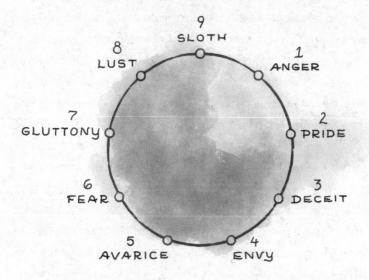

PASSIONS

Type One	Anger
Type Two	Pride
Type Three	Deceit
Type Four	Envy
Type Five	Avarice
Type Six	Fear
Type Seven	Gluttony
Type Eight	Lust
Type Nine	Sloth

For many people, their Enneagram Passion is the fragment of their type to which they subconsciously give permission to lay claim to the whole of their sense of self. For example, some Threes end up believing their own deceptions about how they portray themselves socially and lose sight of the gift of their essence. Some Sixes may be so preoccupied with their fear that they overcompensate by positioning themselves as guardians, losing sight of their other contributions.

It's easy to overidentify with our Passion because it often drives so much of what we do. In fact, when people attempt to self-diagnose their type, the list of Passions often seems most relatable. By accepting our Passion as an intrinsic part of ourselves (or our innate fatal flaw *when* it becomes an addiction), we find confidence in the Enneagram's ability to describe our character structure. But naming and taking responsibility for our Passion is devastating to the ego and can be extremely painful. At the same time, taking ownership of our Passion also leads to tremendous growth. That's why it's fundamentally important that we understand what is meant by the traditional Passions of the Enneagram.

Historically when Christians have tried to translate the Passions, they've wrapped "sin" language around them or overlaid the seven deadly sins* with the capital sins to come up with a list of nine. But frankly, this is a bit of a stretch and has only led us further away from coming home to our True Self.

I've always been a little uncomfortable with the customary alignment of the Enneagram's Passions with notions of sin. Technically the word *passion* comes from the Latin word *passionem* which means "suffering" or "enduring."

Today and throughout history, Christians have used the term

---

* These include anger, envy, gluttony, greed, lust, pride, and sloth. These capital vices or cardinal sins are not listed or identified as the "deadly sins" in Scripture, but were arranged by the desert father Evagrius Ponticus.

passion to describe the suffering of Christ. But if Christ was sinless, then there wasn't any sin in his suffering—unless the connection to the passion of Christ is in relationship to carrying the suffering of the sin of humanity. Even in this reach for meaning we see many prominent theologians now reconsidering atonement theories.

So this brings us to the meaning of the Enneagram's Passions as the ways each type manages and suffers the heart's disconnect from its True Self—the painful emotional experience of enduring the ego's tethering to its tragic flaw. What we are really getting at here is the anguish of having lost contact with our Holy Idea and Virtue.

I'm dominant in type Eight, and so my traditional Passion is lust; however, I would agree with those who clarify its meaning by suggesting it is more accurately a "lust for intensity." So if my type's Basic Fear is of dying, then my lust for intensity is a subconscious attempt to cling to life, to feel truly alive in the purity of innocence. What is sinful about that? What is sinful about trying to reconnect with my True Self or return to my Holy Idea of truth and my Virtue of innocence?

Clearly too much of anything often leads to destructive patterns or addictions, where sin can be found. Certainly our Passions can distort into sin. This is especially true when the consequences of our addictive behaviors catch up to us. I imagine this is what the nineteenth-century American philosopher Elbert Hubbard was suggesting when he wrote, "We are punished by our sins not for them."[1]

In one of my favorite books on the Enneagram, *The Enneagram of Society: Healing the Soul to Heal the World*, Claudio Naranjo does an excellent job explaining the actual sense of the Enneagram's Passions.

Naranjo translates Augustine's notion of sin as it relates to *ignorantia* (ignorance) and *dificultas* (difficulties, distresses, embarrassments) as "a disorder of awareness and an interference with action."[2]

We might think of ignorance as our ego's incomprehension of

our Holy Idea (the mind at rest with its True Self) and of distress as the ego's ache from not living into its Virtue (the heart at rest with its True Self). It is this "disordered awareness" or detachment from our True Self that so often drives our action in destructive ways. Disordered awareness and action are exactly what block the fruit of our Holy Idea and Virtue from being realized, keeping us from our True Self and stuck in sin.

Naranjo goes on to suggest that it may be appropriate to use a sense of pathology, essentially cause and effect, to bring clarity and to "rescue the original sense of the word *sin* that had almost been forgotten after the contamination of the notion of wrongness as a dysfunction with that of wrongness as evil."[3]

This idea advances the question, what do we mean by the Passions, specifically when working with the Enneagram? To differentiate these concepts, Naranjo argues, "The difference between sins and pathologies is, however, the *locus* of responsibility: in so far as 'sin' accuses, making the individual responsible, 'pathology' excuses, making past or present causes beyond the individual responsible. While we are *victims* of mental and interpersonal pathologies, we are *responsible* for our sins."[4]

Both sins and pathologies, of course, cause suffering. This gets to our longing for a reconnection with presence to which our Passions point. The human condition into which we are born gifts us with these Passions for more. "The [P]assions reveal themselves to be a thirst for Being, ultimately based on a loss of contact with the Being."[5]

Regardless of whether the Passions of the Enneagram are more pathologies than sins or tragic flaws, "The King's Diamond," a traditional Jewish parable,* helps us make sense of what is exposed through our understanding of our type.

---

* I first came across this story in Clarence Thomson's *Parables and the Enneagram* and have since seen several other versions. I have done my best to honor the original intent of

Long ago lived a wealthy king whose fortune was unrivaled. He possessed valuable treasures from all known lands including paintings and sculptures from the world's greatest artists. The legend of his prosperity was punctuated by his most prized possession, a precious diamond bigger than any that had ever been seen before. In fact, it was larger than the king's own hand and nearly flawless in its color and clarity.

When the king wasn't admiring it himself, the diamond was put on display for all his loyal subjects to admire—protected by armed guards, of course. Visitors from far and wide came to gaze upon its mythical beauty.

As the king's fame grew and his kingdom flourished, he credited this very special diamond as the source of his prosperity.

One afternoon as the king gazed upon the diamond, holding the precious stone up to the sunlight, to his horror he noticed a deep and long crack from the top of the stone to the very bottom.

"How could this have happened?" he exclaimed, heart-broken with the devastating knowledge that it would be impossible to fix this terrible flaw.

His court gathered around him with his most esteemed advisors attempting to appease his fears. The best jewelers throughout his kingdom visited his throne room to examine the flawed diamond. After inspecting the crack, most were concerned that any attempt to work on the stone would cause further damage, splitting it into countless smaller stones. The only ones to offer solutions suggested cutting the diamond into two new gems which would still be the largest in the land. But the king refused, holding on to an unrealistic hope.

---

the story that is attributed to Jacob ben Wolf Kranz of Dubno.

Finally, a poor, elderly man arrived at the palace and asked if he could examine the stone. Initially the king's guards thought he may be a homeless wanderer but quickly learned he was a gifted lapidary whose engraving artistry was thought to be the best known to humanity.

After scrutinizing the flawed diamond, this old man looked at the king and said, "Your Highness, I know what to do. I can fix this. Not only will I restore its beauty, but I will make it more valuable than you could even imagine." The king sat in disbelief wondering about the audacity of this old man's claims.

"Your Majesty, all I ask is that you let me do my work undisturbed, unmonitored. In two weeks' time I will return your diamond to you. In the meantime, allow your patience and trust to give me the privacy I need to focus on my work."

The king, concerned this might be a con, agreed, adding the condition that the elderly stonecutter must do his work in the palace. A room was prepared and guards appointed to keep watch over the old man's coming and goings. With that, the old man took the stone and began the slow, undramatic work of restoration.

The king couldn't rest, obsessing over the future of his most prized possession.

After two weeks, the old man let the guards know that he was finished with the work and would like to present the diamond to his king. The palace guards rushed to the king's throne room with the most anticipated news of the kingdom, and the court was assembled for the presentation.

Standing before His Majesty, the elderly lapidary held up the diamond, wrapped in a dirty old polishing rag. He carefully pulled the stone from the cloth. There, engraved on the top of the diamond, was an exquisite flower, and the crack down the middle of the stone was its stem.

The king was astonished; the diamond was actually more stunning than before and more beautiful than anyone could have dreamed.

Whether we understand the Enneagram's Passions as sins, sin tendencies, the shape of each type's tragic flaw, or the yearning to return to our True Self, the invitation here is to find the beauty in our imperfections however they manifest themselves.

This is one of the most useful ways to approach the Enneagram, learning to honestly yet compassionately *observe* both our attempts to return home to our True Self and our compulsions that derail us from living into our potential.

Our mind uses the Fixation of our type as a way of convincing our heart that the Passion is justified, creating an inevitable loop of which we must be aware. For example, if the Passion of type Two is pride or, perhaps more accurately, self-abnegation, and the Fixation is flattery, then Twos need to watch for the ways they flatter themselves and the ways their false humility leads to pride. Those dominant in type Seven need to remember that their Passion of gluttony or overdoing what brings them pleasure is kept in play with their Fixation of anticipation—always thinking about what comes next after they've finished feasting on all that their gluttony consumes. This mental and emotional loop of coping doesn't have to control us. Instead, by learning to observe it, we learn to correct its claims on our well-being.

This has been the Enneagram's gift to me.

HOW THE ENNEAGRAM FOUND ME

It was during the summer of 2000, in the slums of Cambodia, that the Enneagram first found me. I met Craig Greenfield, a New Zealander humanitarian and activist living in one of Phnom Penh's poorest neighborhoods. It turns out Craig was my first Enneagram guide. As he explained the Enneagram to me, I was immediately curious but simultaneously suspicious. It made sense, but I resisted being typed until a couple of weeks later when I returned home.

If I'm honest, the symbol itself threw me. It looked *super* evil, like two demonic pentagrams having sex, and I was immediately concerned that it might not be congruent with my Christian faith.

But it had captivated my attention, and I found myself returning to Craig's introduction over and over again. I found several free online tests, took quite a few of them, and then aggregated the various results on a spreadsheet that I emailed to Craig, asking him to help translate what they meant.

From our time together in Cambodia, he already had a sense of my type, so rather than explaining common mistypings or how to understand the various test result methods, he just told me, "I'm pretty sure I know what your type is, but let me ask you this . . . ," and then he posed a question (actually, less a question and more an assumption) about how I relate to my mother.

Somehow, he accurately described a complicated yet subtle dynamic in the way I view and respond to my mom.

I was stunned. Was it that obvious? Could someone really size up all of humanity with just a few inquiries about everyday familial patterns?

I felt exposed, as if he saw right through me. At that moment everything changed for me, and I began seriously exploring the teachings of the Enneagram.

Still, I'd be lying if I said the Enneagram didn't continue to weird me out.

More than once, friends bought me copies of Riso and Hudson's *The Wisdom of the Enneagram*, only for me to quietly return those new copies of the book because much of the interspiritual language felt uncomfortable to me at the time. But the Enneagram is relentless, and once it finds you, it doesn't let go—truth and light are like that. I did give in eventually, delving deeper and deeper into all the material I could find on my type (which is common and what most of us do, but there's so much more to the Enneagram than just the material available about our types).

As is typical of young converts to anything, I started promoting the Enneagram among my friends and professional community. The practical application for interpersonal relationships was transformative. I read many of the classic Enneagram texts, and eventually I had the great honor of being tutored in the Enneagram by my mentor, teacher, and friend Father Richard.

At that time, tragically and of my own doing, I had been bumping around the bottom of life for a while, suffering the consequences of some major life crises created by some unfortunate personal decisions.

After one such humiliation I made a trip to Albuquerque, where I first met Father Richard. Hoping to lean into urgent inner work and much-needed personal restoration, I spent ten days with a few other conversation partners exploring contemplative practices and contemplative spirituality. Father Richard's pastoral care and gentle mentoring further deepened my experience and understanding of spiritual practice.

One day, sitting at a picnic table under New Mexico's hot sun, I shared lunch with Father Richard. I was uncharacteristically quiet. Keenly perceptive, Father Richard recognized the sadness and pain in my eyes and asked if I was okay. My tears fell quietly down my cheeks, and, like I feel with so few others, I knew I was safe with him.

Father Richard wouldn't let me off the hook; he pressed in and asked me why I was there. Hardly answering his question, I broke down. Trying to fight back the tears, I couldn't talk. It was then that

Father Richard's teaching of the Enneagram started with a smile and a gaze that seemed to penetrate my soul with pastoral concern.

After hearing the *why* for my visit, he asked me if I knew my Enneagram type. That was it. That was all he needed to know. In the moments that followed, his smile grew and grew, celebrating the pain I was experiencing as the beginning of good things for me. I didn't understand what he knew nor did I have the ability to truly digest those earliest bits of wisdom he was offering, but I did my best and kept learning.

A couple of years later I once again found myself in New Mexico, but this time in a better place spiritually and emotionally. And that's when Father Richard really let me have it. I spent a week with him, uninterrupted hours absorbing wisdom about the Enneagram I hadn't come across in any of the books. It was absolutely incredible.

Working with the Enneagram for nearly two decades has been transformational. Growing in self-awareness and self-knowledge has changed everything. No doubt it can be devastating to come to terms with our fatal flaws, our characteristic sin tendency, and the primary fear hiding in our subconscious. But awareness of these aspects, or fragments, of our identities is what catalyzes growth.

I'm convinced that approaching the Enneagram from a con-templative posture—a spirituality marked by solitude, silence, and stillness—is the most effective way to work with this character-structure system for whole-person growth and transformation.

Moving beyond the mere discovery of our type's common traits into a deeper exploration that involves learning to discern with our type, facing the temptations and fears of our type, and ultimately praying through our type leads to real inner freedom. And that's when our true identity can be unleashed.

PART

II

EXPLORING
TRIADS *and* TYPES

4

Head, Heart, Body, *and* the Whole Self

Introducing the Intelligence Centers

Most of us are stumped when faced with the question, "How do you hear from God?" Typically, our most common answers point to hearing through others or through experiences, or to waiting on God to acknowledge our consistent and determined investments in a future answer to a prayer we've said.

Some of us think God is speaking outside of us, and so we're always looking for signs or symbols of Divine movement in the world and fail to recognize that we don't need to look outside ourselves to hear from the voice of Love who resides within.

Others think God needs to speak to us from someone else, so we're looking for words from clergy or mentors, conversation partners or friends, books or teachings, and thus miss the good and loving messages that God is already speaking directly to us.

Many of us don't know how to hear from God in the present, so we make the mistake of believing God is somehow waiting for us in the future. This requires that we figure out what's next or how we'll get to where we want to go. But God is here now, closer than our very breath, and can be found in our Intelligence Centers—the

Enneagram's way of helping us recognize our primary mode of perceiving the world through either our head, heart, or body. Each of these Intelligence Centers offers us a different way of experiencing the loving presence and voice of God.

When we are centered, rooted in God's embrace, and present to the God whose name is Love, we realize that we are heard and we can learn to hear. Our Intelligence Centers help us hear and invite us to greater discernment.

So what do we mean by discernment, exactly?

Discernment is our ability to judge what is good, true, and beautiful. Discernment is also the inner knowledge of how to act on that which we perceive. Our use of discernment relies on the clarity of our centered minds, the objectivity of peace-filled hearts, and the unobstructed impulses or instincts* of our bodies.

Frequent invitations to speak about my humanitarian work and lead Enneagram workshops take me all over the world. Most of the venues in which I present are conferences, churches, and campuses. Almost without exception after I speak at a university, a student will approach me and ask about discernment, about how to learn to make good decisions or to trust their judgment. Students aren't the only ones seeking this insight, though; it seems all of us find ourselves questioning our ability to know which voice to listen to and which path to take.

Discernment helps us wade through complicated choices regarding career paths, relationships, where to live, or how to plan for the

---

* While the Holy Ideas rest in the Intelligence Center's harmonious mind and the Virtues rest in the peace-filled heart, the Enneagram's traditional *Instinctual Variants* or *Instinctual Drives* are said to be located in the body. Óscar Ichazo listed them as the Conservation Instinct, the Relations Instinct, and the Syntony Instinct. Today, the Enneagram's instincts are most commonly referenced as Self-Preservation, Sexual, and Social, but when they are referred to as the *Sub-Types*, the Sexual instinct is replaced by "One-to-One." The Enneagram's Instincts are typically ordered from the dominant driving survival strategy to the tertiary or blind spot Instinct. Many believe the Enneagram's Instincts have the strongest defining influence on shaping the differences within people who share the same type.

future. It helps us weigh out new opportunities, their potential as well as their cost.

Discernment also assists us in simpler decision making—for example, learning to say no to social invitations when we're tired and just need some time alone. But when it really seems to count is when we seek to discover our created purpose and how to live into it each moment of each day.

Usually I respond by reminding inquirers that they already know how to practice discernment, and it starts with self-awareness.

I ask them something I learned from an old friend, Jeff Johnson, former BET producer as well as former national director for the NAACP's Youth and College Division: "What makes you cry? What makes you angry? When does your jaw clench or your back straighten?" These kinds of reactions are involuntary physiological responses hardwired into our bodies. We can't help them and have very little control over them. But they're telling us something. As we grow in discernment, we learn to listen to our inner God-given wisdom. And when we learn to tune into the ways God is speaking in us and to us, we are guided into wise living.

Can we learn to listen to God in our minds, trusting the silence underneath the clutter of noise? Can we learn to trust the voice of God that speaks in our hearts, through feelings of pain and peace? Can we learn to sense God at work in our bodies, speaking to us through our resistances and our openness?

I prefer to introduce the Enneagram through the Intelligence Centers rather than through the types because when we learn to trust our primary center, we learn to discern. Listening to thoughts (head), feelings (heart), or instincts (gut) based on your dominant Intelligence Center is the beginning of learning to hear how God has always been speaking to you.

INTRODUCING THE INTELLIGENCE CENTERS

The Enneagram's three Intelligence Centers are the core lenses through which we take in the human experience. They highlight our primary ways of perceiving the world: through our thoughts, our emotions, or our instincts—our head, heart, or body. Each of us leads with one of these in the way we live in the world.

INTELLIGENCE CENTERS

9

8

BODY

1

7

2

HEAD

HEART

6

3

5

4

The Intelligence Centers are the basis for how we perceive ourselves in relationship to our understanding of how the world works and how we work in the world. These centers are activated through our involuntarily physiological reactions and responses to every experience. Growing in familiarity with our primary Intelligence Center is key to helping us develop discernment. Furthermore, matching up an appropriate contemplative prayer posture with our Intelligence Center allows for spiritual alignment and growth.

The Intelligence Centers are one of the many triads found within the Enneagram. They include the Body (instinctive or gut) Center, the Heart (feeling or emotion) Center, and the Head (mind, thinking, or rational) Center. People dominant in type Eight, Nine, or One are located in the Body Center; those dominant in type Two, Three, or Four are clustered in the Heart Center; and those dominant in type Five, Six, or Seven are in the Head Center.

The centers, often referred to as the triadic self, demonstrate the tripartite view of humanity found in the teachings of Plato (concisely tucked into this quote often attributed to him: "Human behavior flows from three sources: desire [body], emotion [heart], and knowledge [head]") and echoed in every major world religion. In this tripartite understanding, the composite of our existence is expressed through three distinct components of the human person, commonly referred to as the body, the soul, and the spirit.

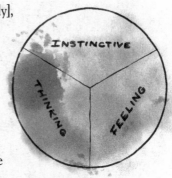

Jesus references this view in his call back to the Hebrew Scriptures' greatest commandment (Deuteronomy 6:5) when he reminds us to "love the Most High God with all your heart, your soul, and your mind" (Matthew 22:37).

This makes sense for those of us who believe that humanity bears a Divine imprint, that we are made in the image of a Triune God.

And so these three core centers connect us to the Divine presence within us that is always guiding and leading through intuition, impulse, and insight.

Learning to observe and listen to these centers is what we generally mean when we speak of discernment. God has already given us everything we need; it's just a matter of recognizing the gifts and accessing them. Our Intelligence Center is the innate gift that indicates how God speaks to us—through our senses and the impressions we experience in our instincts, feelings, and thoughts. These go-to places for each of us are rich spaces that offer clarity in perception, inquiry, and resolution.

What's more, the centers explain something about each of the nine Enneagram types by helping identify a person's most *accessible emotional response* or reaction: *anxiety or distress* for the Head Center, *fear or shame* for the Heart Center, and *frustration or anger* for the Body Center.

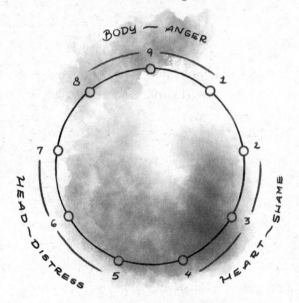

I'm convinced the Intelligence Centers help shape the three levels of consciousness. The conscious mind accesses our thinking or Head Center, allowing for self-reflection and cognitive rationality. The subconscious most readily accesses our feelings or Heart Center, validating our emotions by pointing out the ways they tell us things that our minds can't seem to sort out or explain. The bulk of our unconscious, our instinctual drives, rests in our gut or Body Center, which may be why we carry so much somatic energy that ends up stored as stress or other negative physical sensations or sometimes even illness.

After Phileena and I had been married for twenty years, we finally got a puppy from a pet rescue organization, a sweet little brown dog with a huge heart. We named him Basil. As Phileena puts it, "He rescued us." It turns out an Enneagram Eight like me has a lot to learn from the little guy. He constantly reminds me to be in the present with him, whether we're taking a walk or playing on the rug by our bed, where he's torn apart countless chew toys.

One of Basil's adorable quirks is the way he shakes things off. That funny phrase "shake it off" actually speaks to the body's way of balancing the nervous system. Somehow Basil doesn't need to be reminded of it. He instinctively shakes it off before getting out of bed and starting his day, after being scolded for not following a command, after undergoing a stressful experience on a walk or in the car, or sometimes after spending time with someone he's not so sure about. Basil quietly and quickly gives his little body a rigorous shake to discharge whatever negative energy may have been absorbed.

If only we could learn these simple tricks to return to presence by following our own centers. Just think of all the ways we would be better aligned, better centered, and better able to discern.

THE THINKING TYPES
OF THE HEAD CENTER

Head people, those in the intellectual center, have highly developed mental faculties they use to assess and address everything in life that is experienced as a threat or an assault on their inner state. Head people believe in competency as the cure for instability. Through mastering their environment, head people think they're able to secure their own self-preservation.

HEAD~INTELLECTUAL~THINKING

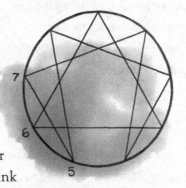

Forecasting helps head people attain a sense of safety. Those dominant in type Five analyze everything to predict the future based on research and a proper understanding of history. Sixes are on constant alert, always attempting to cut off any threat through contingency planning (the kind of person I always want seated in an airplane's exit row since they'll already know there's a problem before the pilots do and will make sure everyone has a chance to get out before the plane goes down). Sevens feel an inner compulsion to maintain access to opportunity as a way of experiencing freedom.

Head people may be the most afraid of their own pain. They think they are unable to emotionally engage their pain through their feelings, so they minimize it. Fives attempt to reduce it as illogical. Sixes consider it another threat that will destabilize their inner sense of security. Sevens are concerned that their pain will limit their freedoms and so they try to reject it entirely.

Fundamentally, head people are obsessed with quieting their inner distress in an effort to create external peace and security. Head people don't have time for the irrational impulses of the instinctive types, nor do they have the patience to truly engage the emotional complexities of the feeling types; rather, they methodically face each of life's problems searching for solutions. Ironically, they often have a hard time activating the answers they discern for the following reasons: Fives generally are concerned that more information is required before coming to a conclusion; Sixes don't trust themselves to formulate correct answers; and Sevens are afraid that answers will bring completion to an internal journey that is unending.

Father Richard explains that in an attempt to cope with their anxiety, "Fives try to master it by gaining more and correct knowledge. [Sixes] link up with an authority or group for security . . . or may take foolish risks or make pre-emptive strikes to overcome their fears. Sevens deny and avoid pain and create fun and fantasy. All three are clever ways of largely living in your head."[1]

THE FEELING TYPES
OF THE HEART CENTER

Heart people are social types who feel their way through life by leaning into their emotional intelligence. Those in the Feeling Center teeter between compulsions for *connection* with others and *comparison* with others to validate their own sense of worth.

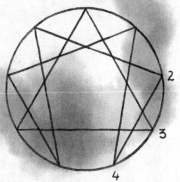

HEART~FEELING~EMOTION

Compared to gut people, those in the Feeling Center are likely to have an overwhelming social presence and are substantially more emotionally present than the other types. However, this emotional presence is also an unconscious coping technique; though heart people can be highly emotionally intelligent, it's not uncommon for them to be out of touch with their *own* feelings or emotional needs. Thus they seek out connection with others as a way to experience their own feelings through the mirroring of others' feelings.

Through affective connections that may seem authentic, heart people externalize their interior fears of not being loved, valued, or seen. At their core they project their fears through quiet attempts to have their own needs met: Twos want to be loved for who they are; Threes are concerned they're more admired than loved; Fours worry there will be no one with the particular ability to love them for what sets them apart as special.

Healthy heart people become a source of love in the world, doing good and bringing balance, but when unhealthy, they lose their sense of self by comparing themselves with others. Twos begin to believe their needs no longer matter, Threes quietly compete with the needs of others, and Fours wallow in their unmet, insatiable needs.

When heart people allow comparison to lead to feelings of disconnection, they blame themselves and can be overcome with profound experiences of shame. Shame in turn produces a sense of fear—the fear that they are unworthy to experience their own needs. This fear is followed by a feeling of even more shame that comes from having needs in the first place.

In an effort to cope with this fear, Father Richard says heart people may "unceasingly develop activities to secure the devotion or attention of others. Twos pose as loveable and helpful, Threes play whatever role 'goes over' best publicly, and Fours put in an appearance as someone special and authentic (to themselves)."[2]

For heart people to practice and grow in discernment means they must learn to trust their feelings. It turns out my younger sister Mendi is dominant in type Two. I remember as a kid hearing adults tell her not to trust her feelings or rely so heavily on her emotions. But people in the Heart Center need to learn that their feelings are telling them something they will have a harder time figuring out in the mind or experiencing in their gut. Discernment for heart types is rooted in their fluency in accessing and trusting their emotional impulses.

THE GUT TYPES
OF THE BODY CENTER

Those in the Body Center are *gut people* who experience life through intuitive instincts and tactile engagement with their senses. People in the instinctive center engage the world through activity in an effort to assert and maintain a sense of their control. Gut people are generally more impassioned than emotional, and their great determination is often the source of their pain.

As gut people ride waves of intensity, instead of shaking it off, they often project their energy onto others as an unconscious way of dissipating the constant static noise of frustration they perpetually experience. By externalizing their interior irritations, gut people assert their desire for control by becoming the solution to the drama they've created: Eights dominate it,

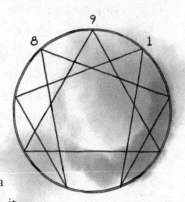

BODY~GUT~INSTINCTIVE

Nines attempt to broker it, and Ones seek to bring back balance by correcting it.

At their best, gut people harness this energy and direct it through their initiating ability to build a better world; at their worst, it seems everything annoys them.

Usually gut people don't know what to do with their feelings. In fact, they tend to dissociate from them. Vulnerable feelings signal to gut people that they may be the source of their own anger, leading to exasperation that somehow they are inherently and irredeemably flawed—a terrifying limiting belief. To avoid such a fear, gut people repress the core emotion so that it is transmuted into impassioned outbursts, typically anger. Coping with fear propels gut people into taking charge of their environment as a diversion tactic to maintain an illusion of control over the consequences created by their anger.

Eights and Ones are more direct—Eights externalize their anger and Ones demonstrate more controlled anger—while Nines are more passive, suppressing their anger until it is finally triggered (often catching themselves and others off guard by it).

Father Richard suggests that those in the Body Center experience life through waves of intensity and "often experience life as *too much,* somewhat like a full body blow to which they develop a characteristic defense: Eights hit back, Nines back off, and Ones try to fix it."[3]

As a gut type myself, I can attest to the constant static noise of frustration that follows nearly every thought or feeling I have. It's most easily detected when I drive; as soon as I'm behind the steering wheel of my little two-door car, it's as if every other driver on the road is trying my last nerve. My impatience and perpetual annoyance are played out in aggressive (not defensive) driving tactics, which only cause unnecessary stress for my passengers, usually Phileena and Basil. Driving really does help me wake up to my frustration, the most accessible emotion of my type, and serves as an invitation to observe its control over me.

THERE'S ALWAYS AN
EXCEPTION TO THE RULE

Now, you may be feeling some resistance to these generalizations about the Intelligence Center triads, especially if you identify as a type Three, Six, or Nine. When drawn, these three types in particular form the equilateral triangle in the center of the Enneagram's circle and have been referred to as the Shock Points (Gurdjieff), the Balance Points (Hurley and Dobson), the Revolutionary Types, or the Anchor Points.

The three Anchor Points (Three, Six, Nine) have perhaps the most archetypal Holy Ideas (the fruit of each type's mental clarity when the mind is connected with the True Self): faith for type Six, hope for type Three, and love for type Nine. You may recall that faith, hope, and love show up at the conclusion of Saint Paul's most poignant declaration about love:

There are, in the end, three things that last: faith, hope, and love. But the greatest of these is love. (1 Corinthians 13:13)

Because these Anchor Points sit in the middle of their Intelligence Centers, neither of their wings reach outside their center. Because their wings don't reach outside their center, they ironically are the most disconnected from their center. The Threes are the most estranged from their hearts (often manifested in their loneliness), the Sixes the most detached from their minds (which explains how irrational they can sometimes be), and the Nines the most disjointed from their bodies (experienced in the ways they calm down their external environments through the mellowing energy they project).

This disconnect from their center makes sense as an internalized coping mechanism because the Anchor Points function as a buffer between the extremes of their wings. Naranjo suggests that type Three is "a polarity of sadness [Four] and happiness [Two] . . . [that Six is] a polarity of aloofness [Five] and expressiveness [Seven] . . . [and Nine] one of amoral or anti-moral [Eight] and over-moral [One]."[4]

To have to bring balance to these polarities internally exhausts the Anchor Points and so in a sense they step back as the referee of the extremes of their wings and, just like any referee, force themselves to become objective observers of the compulsions of their center. Though they demonstrate a pronounced disconnect from their Intelligence Center, they necessarily belong in their triad because they play a crucial role. Part of the inner work invitation for the Anchor Points is to reconnect with their center (head, heart, or gut) and integrate with the other centers for wholeness.

Though the Anchor Points' disconnect from their Intelligence Center is the most obvious exception to the rules of the Enneagram, a couple of less developed and less obvious anomalies also exist.

Humanity's flight, fight, and freeze responses to threatening situations or potential harm can be mapped around the Enneagram's Intelligence Centers. For example, the head types generally flee danger as a result of having thought through the implications of harmful situations. The body or gut types fight back as an instinctive response to control themselves and their environment, another form of domination commonly associated with the gut types. The heart types typically will freeze as a way of staying connected to their hearts and mirroring the hearts of others who also may remain in harm's way.

The Anchor Points, however, provide clear exceptions: they take on the flight, fight, or freeze response of their disintegration path. Threes fight to save face and protect their image; Sixes freeze because they often doubt their inner instincts and natural responses; Nines flee or take flight, which is consistent with their tendency to function in the role of peacemaker, always avoiding confrontation.

Another exception in the Anchor Points is seen in the two pivots of type Six commonly described as the *phobic* Six and the *counterphobic* Six. It's generally accepted that type Six is the only type with two variants. If that's true, however, then this anomaly of the patterns typically observed in the Enneagram contradicts its fractal-like consistency and potentially exposes the Enneagram's thorough consistencies as arbitrary.

I see the Enneagram as a fractal of human character structures, so any irregularity or departure from the observable patterns of the Enneagram creates a dilemma that requires thoughtful investigation. I'd like to suggest that type Six isn't alone in its two variations but that all three of the Anchor Points adapt and fluctuate.

For example, the *phobic* Six, who moves away from their source of fear, is the fraternal twin of the *counterphobic* Six, who presses into whatever it is they are afraid of as a means of overcoming it. Similarly, the *inactive* Nine is prone to prolonged states of apathetic lethargy, sustaining what seems to be a general disinterest, while the fraternal twin is the *overactive* Nine who is an exertive arbitrator, mediating and negotiating as a way of externalizing their own inner dissonance. And finally, the *genuine* Three who never makes even a nominal exaggeration but opts for sincerity in all things is mirrored in their fraternal twin, the *disingenuous* Three, who pretends, impersonates, mimics, and masquerades to attain their goals. Within this theory, the nine types with these three pivots become twelve types, another significant number throughout Scripture (consider, most notably, Jacob's twelve sons who became the fathers of the twelve tribes of Israel, or the twelve disciples Jesus chose to be his first students).

INTEGRATING HEART, HEAD, AND BODY

Though we all have one dominant Intelligence Center, if we become stuck there without integrating the whole of who we are (including all three Intelligence Centers), then we miss the wholeness that is available to us—the wholeness for which we were originally created. For example, if you're a heart type but don't develop fluency in experiencing your gut and head, when you're uncentered or unhealthy, your emotions will be out of sync with who you are. When you are centered in your dominant Intelligence Center, the other two Centers support the dominant one.

Back to *The Wizard of Oz*. If you've seen the film, you'll remember that Dorothy, the young girl from middle America, gets knocked unconscious during a violent storm. While asleep, she falls deep into a dream set in the magical land of Oz, where her task is simply to find her way home. In her dream, Dorothy is joined by three companions who are all searching for something: The Scarecrow is looking for his brain, the Tin Man is looking for his heart, and the Cowardly Lion is looking for his courage.

Traditional Jungian dream analysis teaches that every person or character who shows up in our dreams can be interpreted as a disconnected fragment of our personal unconscious (actually a part of ourselves) trying to get our attention. Essentially, the characters in our dreams represent our inner wisdom trying to sort things out. As a thought experiment, then, what if we applied a Jungian approach to analyzing Dorothy's dream?

If we apply this interpretive lens, it might signify that Dorothy is suffering from a lack of integration with her Intelligence Centers as portrayed by the Scarecrow who needs to connect with his head (the Thinking Center), the Tin Man with his heart (the Feeling Center), and the Cowardly Lion with his courage (the Body Center). Until these parts of Dorothy—these centers—connect, she won't be able to get home and wake up.

And she's aware of this truth the moment she looks at her traveling companions and declares, "It's funny, but I feel as if I'd known you all the time."

If Dorothy continues to stay asleep, her dream (or the illusion she's participating in) will become more and more real to her, distracting and distancing her from the indispensable endeavor of facing reality and living beautifully into its gifts.

In the end, it turns out each of her companions already possessed everything they needed; they just had to come to that revelation for themselves.

That's what we're trying to do here: wake up from the dreams or illusions that often seem more real than our True Self. Dorothy's dream of Oz is filmed in color, while her unintegrated life at home is filmed in black and white. Like Dorothy, sometimes we become so disenchanted by the ordinary that we can't help but create a colorful illusion in which to live. Yet ironically, this fantasy-building only takes us farther from home. The Enneagram, through its unabashed truth-telling, invites us to return to our essential nature, the home for our souls.

Bringing our centers together through the inner work of integration helps us wake up and come home to our True Self. It's a challenging journey but a worthy one. To take the next step, let's take a good, honest look at ourselves in the mirror offered by our Enneagram type.

A Curated Color Wheel
Summary *of* the Nine Types

Finding Yourself within the
Enneagram's Nine Types

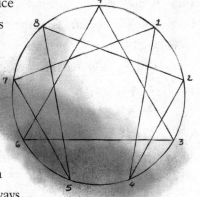

On one of the walls in my office I've hung nine gorgeous hand-carved masks from Ghana, Liberia, Rwanda, Uganda, and other Sub-Saharan African countries. To visitors I sometimes pose the question, "Can you assign each of these masks to one of the nine Enneagram types?" Though their answers always seem to have more to do with an individual's personal interpretation of the nine types, it's nonetheless interesting to hear their rationale for seeing type in the masks that hide true faces.

The first mask I brought back from Africa I purchased at a dusty antique store in Cape Town. I was in South Africa for a large theological conference and needed to escape the windowless convention center to get some fresh air, local food, and a recalibrated perspective.

An old friend of mine wanted to pick up a gift, and so we poked around the heart of the city until we discovered the enchanting vintage gallery where I found the mask. It was hidden away, tucked behind some massive artifacts, but as soon as I saw it I was captivated. Not too big, about the size of a flattened American football, made of dark wood, with long, narrow slots for eyes, tribal markings down the cheekbones and around the chin, and six braids from what looks like actual human hair. Immediately I wanted to get it for my wife Phileena; I'm not sure why, but it felt like there was meaning in it for her.

As I researched the mask's specific design, I learned that it came from the Dan tribe in West Africa and was worn by the woman who served as the intermediary for the young men in her village who were recovering from their rites of passage. After the boys went outside the village for their adolescent circumcision, they weren't allowed back in until they had recovered, so a woman was assigned to check on them each day and to bring them food, water, and medicine if necessary. Essentially the mask was a symbol of nurturing arbitration, accompanying community members who left as children but would return as adults.

What a powerful role this woman must play for her community, helping boys become men, bridging phase-of-life transitions, and reminding these young men that their gateway home was through feminine care as well as feminine strength.

Phileena had played a similar role in our former community for years, helping many of the young men who joined our activist organization to grow up through guided introspection, facilitating their self-care for the longevity of their service, and introducing them to contemplative prayer practices to help ground their social engagement. The mask was a meaningful gift to honor the vocation in which she faithfully served.

But as this role she played was only a small contribution in light of all the others she made, it was like a mask she wore.

Our personality is the mask we wear—it is part of us but not the whole. Some of the masks we wear are formed for us by our environment and upbringing, some we forge through the mythology of our own ego projections, and some are unfairly put on us by society as caricatures. Regardless of where they come from, it's up to us to determine how long we'll wear them.

Unfortunately, our tendency is to overidentify with some of the masks we put on. Some of us feel stuck in our pasts, suffocated by shame or guilt, racked by disappointment or regret, overcome by fear or doubt. The first mistake we make is misinterpreting these voices in our heads and hearts as the voice of God (though God is never as hard on us as we are on ourselves). Our second mistake is giving away our power to the toxic and destructive control that the pains of our past hold over us. And the last mistake we make is allowing those we've hurt or let down to fasten these masks to us in ways that make us feel we'll never be able to get them off.

Learning to see ourselves for who we truly are—the good, the bad, the ugly—is a gift of grace. The Enneagram helps us do just that.

UNFOLDING THE MAP

Discovering our type is the key to opening the sacred Enneagram, and once opened, our sense of self begins to make sense. As we unfold this soul map, it's as if everything we've intuitively known about ourselves is exposed right there before us.

Usually when someone first begins learning about the Enneagram, they do an internet search or find a book and immediately turn to the chapter on their type. The components used to describe type usually include the type's Holy Idea, Virtue, Childhood Wound, Basic Desire, Basic Fear, Passion, and Fixation. But how are all these fragments of character structure related?

A couple of years ago I developed a drawing I use to chart just that—the relationships between each Enneagram type's intrinsic elements. Think of it as the map key. I took some liberty and mixed up the language a bit, using *Original Virtue* for True Self (which includes the Holy Idea and Virtue), *Attack on Virtue* for Childhood Wound, *Virtue Intention* for Basic Desire, *Virtue Compulsion* for Basic Fear, and *Virtue Addictions* to describe the Passions and Fixations loop.

VIRTUE STRUCTURE

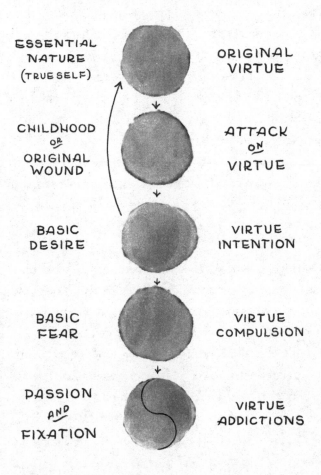

ESSENTIAL NATURE (TRUE SELF)	ORIGINAL VIRTUE
CHILDHOOD or ORIGINAL WOUND	ATTACK ON VIRTUE
BASIC DESIRE	VIRTUE INTENTION
BASIC FEAR	VIRTUE COMPULSION
PASSION AND FIXATION	VIRTUE ADDICTIONS

I deliberately emphasize Virtue because when we do return to our essence, the impression of the Virtue is what is most evident to ourselves and others. Our Virtue is the lingering fragrance of our essential purity; it is what makes each of us beautiful. Sadly, the messiness of our human condition makes us feel distant from our Virtue.

Of course, returning to our Virtue is familiar, like a homecoming, because it is who we have always been. It's who we are, untainted by life's harms and untangled from our anxieties and addictions, free and clear of the fears and misdirected behaviors that get us so off track and cause us to be disconnected from home, lost.

The illustrated Virtue Structure (see preceding page) reveals the map key within the map—uncovering the way each of us has lost our True Self. After all, if we can identify how we lost our way, we're more likely to discover the way back home.

Original Virtue = True Self or Our Essential Nature

On the Enneagram we can map where we've come from, the departure from our essence, that original innocence we experienced in the early days of our infancy when the world actually might have seemed okay. Though we didn't possess the psychological framework to describe our experience of self, we clung to the memory of our essence, hoping to retain that sense of adequate or sufficient power and control, security and survival, affection and esteem.*

	Holy Ideas	Virtues
Type One	Holy Perfection	Serenity
Type Two	Holy Will, Freedom	Humility
Type Three	Holy Harmony, Hope	Truthfulness, Authenticity

---

* Thomas Keating's traditional "programs for happiness."

Type Four	Holy Origin	Equanimity, Emotional Balance
Type Five	Holy Transparency	Detachment
Type Six	Holy Strength, Faith	Courage
Type Seven	Holy Wisdom	Sobriety
Type Eight	Holy Truth	Innocence
Type Nine	Holy Love	Action

Attack on Virtue = Childhood Wound

But something happened, as it always does, and a jarring from our essence took place—an attack on the Holy Idea and Virtue of our True Self. The impact of our Childhood Wound changed everything. Perhaps our caregiver's love wasn't enough, or maybe an actual physical or emotional wound scarred our psyche. Our Childhood Wound jolted us into the pain of humanity and forced us to fall asleep, because sleeping became easier and seemingly safer than facing reality.

In our slumber we lost ourselves, forgot who we really were—just like in Oz where Scarecrow forgot he had a brain, Tin Man forgot he had a heart, and Lion forgot he had courage. Whatever this wound was, it was a full-out attack on our essence, a theft of our True Self. This wound sent us down our own Yellow Brick Road in search of healing.

Virtue Intention = Basic Desire

The attack on our essence created within each of us what I call Virtue Intention, which is simply our Basic Desire or drive to wake up, to get back home.

As with Dorothy from *The Wizard of Oz*, each person's Basic Desire is the unique way they want to get "home." It is the ego's yearning to return to its essence. It is the soul's desire to reconnect with its original righteousness. The Basic Desire is the primary motivation of the

Enneagram type's unconscious aspiration to return to centered presence or True Self. Each of us has a Basic Desire, the way we attempt to return to our True Self. We spend much of our lives driven by this intention, this Basic Desire to come out of our slumber and remember who we are.

Because there's "no place like home," as Dorothy says when she clicks those iconic ruby slippers, we just want to find our way back there, back to that snapshot in our human experience when all was well.

	Basic Desire
Type One	To be good, to have integrity
Type Two	To feel love
Type Three	To feel valuable
Type Four	To be themselves
Type Five	To be capable and competent
Type Six	To have support and guidance
Type Seven	To be satisfied
Type Eight	To protect themselves
Type Nine	To have peace of mind and wholeness

Virtue Compulsion = Basic Fear

But our Basic Desire, a good and holy drive in and of itself, too often becomes warped by our insecurities and doubts that we can ever find our way home. This mentality feeds into our Basic Fear—that we'll never return to our True Self and that we'll stay stuck in the dream, just as Dorothy got stuck in Oz. This fear is experienced as a compulsion, thus our "Virtue Compulsion." Like all fears, it is only as powerful as we allow it to be. But like all fears, it clouds our vision of our True Self and our way home.

Those in each Enneagram type have an underlying dread that their Basic Desire is unrealistic or can't be met. Like Dorothy fearing she'll never get home once the Wizard flies away in his hot-air balloon without her, each type's Basic Fear is that they are stuck in their flawed human experience, trapped in the consequences of their Childhood Wounds. It's the fear that reconnecting with the essence of the True Self is impossible.

	Basic Fear
Type One	Of being bad, imbalanced, defective, corrupt
Type Two	Of being unloved
Type Three	Of being worthless, without inherent value
Type Four	Of having no identity or significance
Type Five	Of being helpless, incompetent, and incapable
Type Six	Of being without support and guidance
Type Seven	Of being trapped in pain and deprivation
Type Eight	Of being harmed, controlled, and violated
Type Nine	Of being lost, separated, and fragmented

Virtue Addictions = Passion + Fixation

To deal with this fear and the consequences of the attack on our essence, we appeal to our coping addictions: (1) Passions—how each type manages its loss of presence, or how the heart suffers its disconnect from its True Self, and (2) Fixations—the mental tactics used to convince an uncentered mind that its Passion is legitimate.

Within the larger Sacred Enneagram, the Virtue Structure casts light on what can seem like a dark and obscure path on the journey home.

Once we understand how the components of type relate to one

another we begin to see the "why" behind our types. Let's examine this Virtue Structure as an overlay to each of the nine types, moving beyond mere caricature of personality traits to the drives behind type.

	Passion	Fixation
Type One	Anger	Resentment
Type Two	Pride [Self-Abnegation]	Flattery
Type Three	Deceit	Vanity
Type Four	Envy	Melancholy
Type Five	Avarice	Stinginess
Type Six	Fear	Cowardice
Type Seven	Gluttony	Planning
Type Eight	Lust	Vengeance
Type Nine	Sloth	Indolence

TYPE ONE

Holy Idea	Holy Perfection
Virtue	Serenity
Basic Desire	To be good, to have integrity
Basic Fear	Being bad, imbalanced, defective, corrupt
Fixation	Resentment
Passion	Anger
Direction of Integration	Type Seven
Direction of Disintegration	Type Four*

Ones are ethical and principled, a source of goodness and virtue in the world; they elevate the standard of excellence for quality and integrity in all things.

As mentioned earlier, Ones have an internal drive to be perfect that is rooted in their characteristic Childhood Wound: "These children felt heavily criticized, punished, or not good enough. Household rules may have felt inconsistent. As such they became obsessed with being good/not making mistakes to avoid condemnation. The principal message was: 'You must always be better than you are'"[1] Because of the real or perceived experience that the rules defined their sense of inner goodness, Ones cling to their adherence to rules as a security blanket—an ever-present symbol of their frustration with the world's (and their own) imperfections.

The wound of never being able to measure up fortified their Basic Fear that they are somehow inherently corrupt. That fear fuels their constant frustration with things, which is transmuted through anger, the traditional Passion of the One. But the anger of the One isn't rage so much as the exasperating annoyance that everything around them (and more intensely, everything inside them) is flawed. And tragically, they put unrealistic pressure on themselves to be the one to fix and correct it all. This constant frustration with all that has gone awry is immediately obvious to them, and what's amiss about anything is usually the first thing they notice.

---

* The type components listed in each of the following nine sections are Óscar Ichazo's traditional framing of each type and are taken from The Enneagram Institute's "RH Enneagram At-a-Glance Chart 1: Personality Elements" based on *Understanding the Enneagram* by Don Riso and Russ Hudson, © 2006, The Enneagram Institute.

Perhaps hardest for Ones is the way they continually disappoint themselves and their own inner standards—so the frustration they have with the external world is first practiced and perfected on their inner lives. This inner frustration is frequently communicated in ways that come across as judgmental. What's important to remember is that the judgment Ones levy on the outside world has already been levied inwardly, so the sense of judgment isn't hypocritical.

The critical way they sometimes come across may wear thin with people in relationship with Ones, but it actually should invite compassion when we realize that Ones criticize themselves from the moment they wake up every day. The veracity with which they criticize themselves is unexplainably fiercer than the rest of us could imagine. Just think of all the energy Ones expend as they constantly strive to be better, the pressure they feel as they assume too much responsibility for everyone's work, and their persistent fear of criticism for not meeting expectations. Imagine how difficult life is for the One who just wants to be good, who just wants to do their best (probably better than their best), who just wants to live in a peace-filled world that is good and where people are treated fairly.

If the Passion of the One is anger, then the traditional Fixation of the One is resentment. Ones resent themselves first (this is true for all types; each of us aims the energy of our Fixation internally first, perfecting the negative impressions of it on our own egos before transmuting it externally), feeling that they know better or that in every situation they could have done better. Because of their flaws they beat themselves up, second-guessing the words they used in conversation, for example, or fretting about the quality of work they presented at school or to their employers; just about every decision they make throughout the day is internally interrogated and found to be wanting.

The resentment that Ones direct at themselves keeps them in the anger-resentment loop, always mad at themselves for not measuring up, always resentful that they could have done better. This resentment is what shapes the One's social tendencies, rooted in their sense of duty. Their dutiful compliance isn't so much a social style in relationships as it is compliance to their superego or inner critic (which for Ones is the toughest of all Enneagram type inner critics).

Ones are also idealists, clinging to the notion that a perfect world is possible, but they are the problem because they can't align themselves with their own ideals of perfection.

When a One leans into their Nine wing, we see how their eye for virtue is really a drive to reconcile all things, be they sacred or mundane. With a developed Nine wing, Ones learn to be understanding and accepting of themselves and others. As Ones lean into their Two wing, they view their drive for excellence as a gift to be granted to others, an offering of integrity to the world.

In their path toward integration, Ones are drawn into the playful energy of the Seven, and their imaginations are sparked and their dreams renewed. As they borrow the positive traits of the Seven, they let themselves off the hook and are some of the most winsome of all the Enneagram types.

When they lose themselves and start to bump around the bottom of life, not getting their way by imposing unrealistic standards, Ones disintegrate toward the Four. In disintegration, Ones believe their own lie that they alone are the only ones who understand and value excellence—that no one else has the capacity to grasp what is required for goodness to be actualized in the world.

Finally, when Ones learn to rest and open themselves to undeserved grace, their Virtue of serenity blossoms. Centered Ones reflect integrity and goodness, and the peacefulness with which they offer those things is disarming and inviting.

TYPE TWO

Holy Idea	Holy Will, Holy Freedom
Virtue	Humility
Basic Desire	To feel love
Basic Fear	Being unloved
Fixation	Flattery
Passion	Pride
Direction of Integration	Type Four
Direction of Disintegration	Type Eight

As a source of love in the world, the openheartedness of Twos is rooted in their essence, their True Self. Twos are gracious and generous, naturally giving of themselves, usually in the most befitting ways.

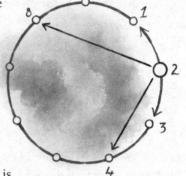

Twos find themselves navigating a fear of being rejected in their relationships. This fear of rejection is, in a sense, an echo of the pain they felt from an experience of feeling rejected by their protective caregiver. As a coping technique, they assume overly nurturing roles in their relationships.

Because their Childhood Wound involves the pain of trying to suppress their own needs, Twos experience deep shame when forced to acknowledge their own needs or ask for their needs to be met. Frequently Twos will take whatever they can get, convincing themselves that even if they're not being loved the way they want or need, at least they're receiving something.

Getting Twos to be honest about what they really need can cause them tremendous stress. Twos ache, their hearts always breaking for the needs they intuitively recognize in those around them. This ache, however, can be a distraction that keeps them from looking inward at what they want and need. When they do recognize their own needs, their ache is replaced with a new kind of pain as they question whether they really are loved. Frequently Twos will ask those with whom they're in relationships, "Do you *really* love me?" Such a question inevitably comes as a surprise since Twos are often the most lovable of all Enneagram types.

Traditionally, the Basic Fear of the Two is living in a world without love, but perhaps more accurately, it is the fear that they aren't loved for *who they are* but only for what they give others.

The traditional Passion of the Two is pride, which can be deceiving because the pride of the Two is more like false humility or, even more specifically, self-abnegation. Self-abnegation as the denial of their own needs causes Twos to put everyone else's needs first. The pride of self-abnegation is fortified by the traditional Fixation of the Two, flattery.

I find this best characterized by Shel Silverstein's book *The Giving Tree*, which tells the beautiful yet tragic story of a little boy who loved an apple tree, and the ways the apple tree loved the boy in return. As a child, the boy climbed and played on the tree; as an adolescent, he picked and sold the tree's apples for income; as an adult, he cut the limbs of the tree to build himself a home; and after being away a long time, he returned sad, wanting to flee his pain, and so he used the trunk of the tree to make a boat to escape.

After each of these snapshots of the tree's selflessness, the repeating line "and the tree was happy" punctuates the story.

Finally, the boy returns as an elderly man, and the heartbroken tree laments she has nothing to offer: her apples, branches, and trunk are gone. But the man, now old and tired, only needs a place to rest. So he takes a seat on what is left of the tree, just a humble stump, which the tree readily offers, and the book closes with the self-flattering line, "and the tree was happy."

Any relationship that resembles the one found in *The Giving Tree* needs to be thoroughly condemned as disgusting in the ways it fortifies entitlement at the expense of the one who gives. "And the tree was happy" perfectly captures the aching heart of the Two, whose pride in being able to give something covers the lie of how she denied her own needs and allowed herself to be taken from. The flattery of Twos convinces them that diminishing themselves through self-abnegation is a legitimate form of love.

Twos who lean toward their One wing follow their principles in the ways they serve others and often come across as more serious than Twos with a strong Three wing, who appeal to their generous nature to draw more attention to themselves or those they serve.

At their best, Twos integrate to the Four, asserting themselves by taking back their power and differentiating themselves from those they love. Integrated Twos may find themselves tapping into their inner creativity as an act of loving service fueled by their notions of beauty.

In disintegration Twos take on the Eight's manipulative tricks, appealing to their own force of presence to get what they want; Twos do this by becoming overly smothering or overly involved, and when they don't feel appreciated they can also become overly controlling.

When Twos can be honest about their own needs, let their needs be met without feeling shame, and allow themselves to receive love in the ways they need it, their Virtue humility shines forth. Virtuous Twos stand with their heads high, take ownership of themselves, and give of themselves from a place of strength and determination as the fruit of deep humility.

TYPE THREE

Holy Idea	Holy Harmony, Holy Law, Holy Hope
Virtue	Truthfulness, Authenticity
Basic Desire	To feel valuable
Basic Fear	Being worthless
Fixation	Vanity
Passion	Deceit
Direction of Integration	Type Six
Direction of Disintegration	Type Nine

At a fundamental level, Threes reflect truth and integrity, because in their essence they know they are truly loved. But Threes live out of the pain of the disconnect from their own hearts, constantly questioning the fragile line between being loved and being recognized or affirmed as the symbol of love they are desperate for.

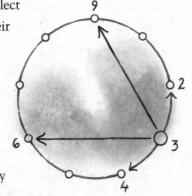

In their Childhood Wound, Threes lost themselves behind the attention they received for their performance; they didn't know from what their value derived, and so they went in search of validation by attempting to avoid any form of failure. This misguided quest upset not only their experience of being loved but, at the core, the reasons why love is offered.

The malformation of selfless love makes it difficult for Threes to accept unmerited or unearned expressions of affection or attention.

Their quietly competitive nature is rooted in their inner drive to prove to themselves that they are valuable. This inner drive is perpetuated by the Basic Fear of the Three, that somehow they are hopelessly worthless and characteristically base.

Hoping to feel love in the emptiness of their hearts, Threes play roles in order to be appreciated, admired, and valued. They are constantly looking for external affirmation to help convince them that they can accept themselves as noble and true.

Traditionally, the Passion of the Three is deceit, but Threes generally aren't liars—in fact, Threes recognize their own capacity to be a source of truth and have an innate ability to sniff out those who would misrepresent themselves, live behind exaggerations, or be untrustworthy. The deceit of the Three is expressed in their ability to pivot or flex and assume any role, position, or opinion required to accomplish whatever they want to achieve. It's a chameleon-esque ability to make connections in order to quell their inner hunger for recognition. And they *will* achieve whatever they set their hearts to.

Threes instinctively connect to nurturing expressions of love in their childhood and carry the ability to self-nurture forward into their adult lives.

Everything that pragmatic Threes set out to do has practical implications for advancing their notions of success that functionally support their desire to feel accepted and loved.

One of the Anchor Points located in the middle of the Feeling Center, Threes are the most disconnected from their own hearts and often the most distant of all Enneagram types from their own dreams, feeling an internal drive to accomplish the unrealized dreams of their caregiver(s).

Not necessarily prone to introversion, Threes sometimes are perceived as detached while still assertive in their social environments. Their reservation allows them to keep enough distance from people to read the subtext and find ways to relate to or work with those they intend to guide or lead.

Though frequently leading, surprisingly Threes aren't always the visible or dominant leaders. Threes find ways to lead through unassuming or less-than-obvious ways, ultimately getting what they want by coming at challenges from a variety of starting points—but conscious of the destination they're aiming for.

With a strong Two wing, Threes can be overly charming and incredibly present both socially and emotionally. With a Four wing, Threes become uniquely specialized in their vocational commitments, giving themselves to hard work in yet another attempt to be recognized and validated.

When Threes integrate to Six, they become less focused on themselves or their carefully curated images, instead centering on the success of their loved ones or communities as a means of securing stability and security for all.

In disintegration Threes fall backward into unhealthy manipulative surrenders, giving up as a way of making peace without feeling like they've lost. Yet these concessions are merely a way of giving up and giving in, which makes everyone feel as if no one has really won anything.

The traditional Virtue of the Three is authenticity, demonstrated in their sincere warmth, genuine concern, and truthful integrity. The centered Three brings forward significance and beauty in all they accomplish or set out to accomplish.

TYPE FOUR

Fours are a natural source of significance. But of all the types, Fours may be the most misunderstood, as evidenced in the way they are frequently depicted in much of the Enneagram literature.

Holy Idea	Holy Origin
Virtue	Equanimity, Emotional Balance
Basic Desire	To be themselves
Basic Fear	Having no identity or significance
Fixation	Melancholy
Passion	Envy
Direction of Integration	Type One
Direction of Disintegration	Type Two

The irony is that Fours feel more misunderstood and less significant than all the other types, even though they are generally considered to be the most uniquely interesting Enneagram type.

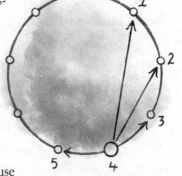

It's not uncommon for Fours to feel beaten down by negative caricatures of their personality quirks, because simply describing personality traits misses the point. Fours know they are different. And because they feel exceptional, they believe most of the rules don't apply to them; they can see an exception in nearly every scenario where a precedent has been set.

The customary Childhood Wound of the Four is found in their experiences of disconnect or distance from their caregiver(s). Their wound and the subsequent ways it caused them to turn in on themselves are the reason behind the Four's feelings of abandonment. This sense of wounding only reinforces their Basic Fear: that they have no personal importance or somehow are less significant than others.

Feeding off the pain of these early experiences with their caregiver(s), Fours fuel their own idealism, which causes a deep frustration that they can never truly find themselves apart from others. Accordingly, it's frequently suggested that Fours are constantly looking to be rescued by someone who can see them for who they truly are.

Fours can be guilty of oversharing their pain and angst or, conversely, repressing it or hiding it, which leads to further isolation and pain.

Fours ache to be understood. They deeply desire to be known. They are perpetually in search of their own significance, which is why they have such a highly developed ability to see beauty in all things. The very thing they are looking for within, they can easily see everywhere else. Thus their intuitive ability to see beauty is tragically wasted on themselves because they tend to overidentify with their flaws and believe that's why they don't belong or fit in.

The traditional Passion of Fours is envy, but not the kind that is aimed at someone else's possessions. Instead, their envy is in their longing for the substance that they think lies behind others' meaningful experiences in their most intimate relationships, or in their perception of others' satisfaction in life's deepest experiences.

Fours chase after what they perceive others have, and when they finally arrive at these idealized destinations, they are left empty because no experience for Fours can ever be more than a hollow shell of the unrealistic expectation they set it up to be.

This addiction to fantasizing is the traditional Fixation of the Four. Longing and fantasizing create a painful loop of constant dissatisfaction and frustration, which is why Fours often feel trapped in darkness while they suffer deep sadness and discontent.

Personally expressive, emotionally sensitive, and keenly self-conscious, Fours with a Three wing allow their pain to drive them into particularly creative vocations where success points back to their unique contributions.

With a Five wing, Fours appear more withdrawn, detaching from external pursuits and opting for more esoteric, mental arenas where they use lucid imagination and creativity to explore who they want to become.

Fours integrate to the One. Fours in integration start to understand that rules and regulations do in fact apply to them as well. Reaching toward type One, Fours have a deep knowing that their messy exaggerations of their longings need boundaries to be healthy, and that structure can be a container of self-discovery just as ambiguity is.

In disintegration Fours give themselves away like an unhealthy Two, appealing to toxic emotional fusion in an attempt to draw the attention they desire.

Awakened Fours bring forward the traditional Virtue of equanimity, or balance—not allowing themselves to be swept up by their strong feelings and deep pains, but resting in even-minded, balance-hearted composure and clarity.

TYPE FIVE

Holy Idea	Holy Omniscience, Holy Transparency
Virtue	Detachment
Basic Desire	To be capable and competent
Basic Fear	Being helpless, incompetent, and incapable
Fixation	Stinginess
Passion	Avarice
Direction of Integration	Type Eight
Direction of Disintegration	Type Seven

Fives illuminate what can be known and are a source of wisdom and knowledge in a world of questions and uncertainty.

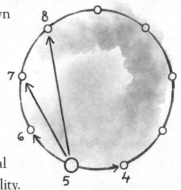

Type Five is perhaps the most withdrawn of all the Enneagram types, their withdrawal a means of finding the mental and cerebral room to understand and master reality. Fives are intrinsically afraid they don't possess the capacity within themselves to distinguish reality or assess what is fundamentally real. This explains the Basic Desire of type Five, which is to uncover the essence of truth. Without the clarity of an answer, who is the Five but a lost wanderer in search of safety?

Fives experience a Childhood Wound that is often explained around the loss of boundaries caused by intrusions from their care-giver(s). To cope with the pain of feeling confused or unable to find resolution (especially in relationships), Fives are suspicious of most attempts to love and nurture them as emotional distractions that they can't trust. And so they withdraw even deeper into the curious places of their minds and imaginations.

As much as Fives love to learn, they often don't need teachers because lectures tend to be presented too slowly for the pace of the Five's mind. Learning with teachers also requires them to expend some of their social energy, which can be distracting to a Five's learning process.

Fives may appear aloof or absentminded, but just the opposite is true. The mental thought processes of Fives are constantly churning through questions to be deciphered and answers to be discovered.

Minimalists on the exterior, Fives have an interior life as complex as any Enneagram type—this is the great misunderstanding of Fives, especially for those who don't have close relationships with people dominant in type Five.

The traditional Passion of the Five is avarice, a form of greed, yet when Fives choose their friends they are far from greedy. In fact, Fives are frequently generous, thoughtful, and surprisingly present in their closest relationships. The avarice or greed of the Five has to do with their withholding of energy, specifically the energy they have for social interactions. This is their way of protecting their mental space from intrusions that feel like invasions. Fives feel worn out by the perpetual analysis and questioning of their theorizing and investigations, so protecting their energy is a priority.

The traditional Fixation of the Five is stinginess, which fuels the disengagement they are accused of. The stinginess of the Five is really their ability to keep from giving more externally than they feel they can give themselves internally.

Fives with Four wings have a propensity for thoughtful curiosity, and they frequently give themselves to niche sorts of jobs that require a developed ability to process nuances and differences.

With a Six wing, the Five can use their inquisitive acumen to solve nearly any problem as a way of establishing security by arriving at answers.

Frequently misunderstood, Fives move to the Eight in integration, finally showing up and asserting what they know to be true by dispelling the fuzziness of exaggerations or inaccuracies based on opinions or force of personality.

Most surprising is a Five in disintegration who moves to the Seven, taking on the manipulation techniques associated with gluttony and excess. Fives who can't figure out an answer, find a solution, or get to the bottom of an intellectual problem simply give up and let themselves go. Frustrated with their inability, they turn to coping techniques such as overconsumption of alcohol or drug abuse, overeating, overactivity, or other unhealthy and addictive patterns that help them numb their pain and dull the sharpest edges of their minds.

Additionally, it is said that the Virtue of the Five is detachment, but maybe more accurately the growth pattern for someone dominant in type Five is the move from detachment to nonattachment in its purest form.

Letting go of the drive to find answers and solutions, letting go of the compulsion to solve problems, and letting go of the need to understand everything enables Fives to rest in the glory of mystery, allowing all that is to simply be.

TYPE SIX

Holy Idea	Holy Strength, Holy Faith
Virtue	Courage
Basic Desire	To have support and guidance
Basic Fear	Being without support and guidance
Fixation	Cowardice
Passion	Fear
Direction of Integration	Type Nine
Direction of Disintegration	Type Three

At their best, Sixes are a source of determination and strength. Often Sixes doubt themselves, looking to an external authority or outside sources to remind them what they hope (and fundamentally know) is true about themselves. Constantly reaching outward to fortify what they need to be able to trust inward keeps the Six stuck in anxious places of uncertainty.

As the Anchor Point of the Thinking Center, Sixes rest in the middle of the intellectual Intelligence Center. They are thought to be the most disconnected from their thoughts and can be the most irrational of all the Enneagram types.

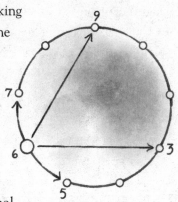

The Childhood Wound of the Six is framed around an experience of inner doubting based on external threats that caused them to feel unsafe. This experience led young Sixes to attach to the protective energy of their caregiver(s), and as a result, Sixes take on protective instincts throughout their lives, always on the lookout for threats.

As Sixes perpetually navigate their apprehensions, their Basic Fear is that they will be lost or won't have the support they need to find their way. Sixes are constantly concerned they will lose their sense of grounded orientation. This fear drives Sixes to ensure that they have the support structures, systems, and leadership required to feel safe.

When Sixes feel threatened, afraid, or unsure about their leaders or authorities, they might gather in small groups of confidants where they feel they can safely vent or process their anxiety, reassuring themselves that their concerns are valid. Unfortunately, such groups may be perceived as mutinous—especially when they are driven by the anxiety of a Six. Frequently these small groups end up overthrowing or securing the removal of leadership or the support structures that are the source of a Six's doubt. What might be surprising in these scenarios is that in many cases the Six does not actually want to assume leadership. Sure, Sixes make great leaders, but because they're constantly second-guessing themselves, healthy Sixes know when they should or shouldn't assume leadership roles. When they work to remove existing support structures, they only intend to create opportunities for adequate or trustworthy leadership to replace that which they perceive to be a threat.

The traditional Passion of the Six is fear, which is experienced as anxiety, angst, or irrational overthinking processes. The traditional Fixation is cowardice, the self-doubting loop that keeps Sixes trapped in their anxious fear.

Sixes with a Five wing take excellent care of those whom they love. They step up to care for their friends and community by establishing stability as a defense against the threats they continually imagine.

Sixes with a Seven wing are tested and true companions, loyal friends who will never fail to show up. Their Seven wing ensures relational presence that meets the needs of the people in their lives through sincerity and generosity. When you are in the good graces of a Six and have earned their trust, there is no better friend. Always faithful, always supportive, always caring.

Incredibly pragmatic, Sixes can be entirely sensible and confident in the way they live, even in the face of tremendous inner doubt.

In their integration Sixes borrow the positive traits of type Nine, leveraging their intuitive threat forecasting skill as a means of brokering a more peaceful world and learning to mitigate the anxiety in themselves and become more peace-filled.

When Sixes disintegrate toward type Three, they find themselves overworked in an attempt to calm their inner distress, thinking if only they gave more effort they would find the safety and stability they are so afraid of losing.

The traditional Virtue of the Six is courage, and no type is stronger or more resilient than a rooted and centered Six.

TYPE SEVEN

Holy Idea	Holy Wisdom, Holy Work, Holy Plan
Virtue	Sobriety
Basic Desire	To be satisfied
Basic Fear	Being trapped in pain and deprivation
Fixation	Planning
Passion	Gluttony
Direction of Integration	Type Five
Direction of Disintegration	Type One

Sevens, the most energetic of all Enneagram types, are a source of imagination and freedom in the world.

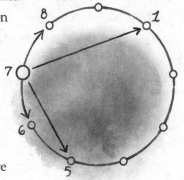

Due to their charming and winsome energy, Sevens are often mistaken as feeling types. Because they come across as very heart-forward, they are frequently assumed to be in their hearts, but Sevens are actually rooted in the Head Center.

Their fundamental need is to avoid pain, so Sevens are perpetually looking for distractions and opportunities to stay as far away as possible from their inner aches.

The Childhood Wound of a Seven was experienced in relationship to the nurturing energy of their caregiver; they felt frustrated because they weren't nurtured enough, always needing more. And so Sevens take on a self-nurturing posture as a means of coping with their residual pain and frustration.

The Basic Fear of the Seven is of dispossession and deprivation. Scarcity of options and opportunity creates tremendous anxiety for Sevens. They are terrified of being stuck with their own pain, so they stay overly active to stave off the inner ache they desperately and frenetically avoid facing. Their fear compels them to chase after their lucid imaginations, like a small child trying to capture a butterfly, not realizing the near impossibility of the task.

People misunderstand Sevens by suggesting they typically lack the ability to follow through with all the amazing things they give themselves to. This misunderstanding is rooted in the value that Sevens place on freedom. To bring closure to anything forces limitations on the freedom they seek to establish in their own lives and create for others. Always positive, always hopeful, voraciously curious, Sevens remind us all that we are alive.

As mentioned earlier, Sevens are in their heads, using their mental faculties to think forward and plan what's next. You can test this by asking a Seven about their most spectacular failures. Things that other types would beat themselves up over for days if not months or years, Sevens can sleep off, waking up the next morning having easily put the past behind them and ready to think about what's next.

The traditional Passion of the Seven is gluttony, but this can be misleading since many Sevens don't simply overeat. The gluttony of the Seven is their determination to overdo everything that brings them gratification—feasting on options and opportunities until they are overwhelmed by their indulgences and sickened by their excessive addiction to pleasure.

The traditional Fixation of the Seven is planning, constantly anticipating what they will do next, fearful that when the current pleasure they've given themselves to has come to an end, they too will come to their own end.

Sevens with a Six wing draw people in, using their charisma

to establish reassurance in relationship. By offering spontaneity, they take others on "mini-vacations" from their own life dramas or problems, giving their friends a much-needed break by allowing the positive outlook of the Seven to help reframe any situation.

Sevens with an Eight wing are determined, more realistic, more driven, and a little more serious, yet still inquisitive, leaning into the drive of the Eight to push the boundaries even further.

In integration Sevens move toward the Five, growing in mental clarity and learning restraint.

In disintegration Sevens can seem hypocritical, appealing to the rigid and unrealistic standards of Ones as a means of justifying themselves as more tempered than their critics. But that's never the case in their disintegration.

When Sevens can find their grounding in their Virtue, sobriety emerges. In their sobriety, Sevens show tremendous control, develop highly attuned discernment skills to regulate their excesses, and are luminaries of restraint despite their insatiable inner drive for pleasure.

TYPE EIGHT

Holy Idea	Holy Truth
Virtue	Innocence
Basic Desire	To protect themselves
Basic Fear	Being harmed, controlled, and violated
Fixation	Vengeance
Passion	Lust
Direction of Integration	Type Two
Direction of Disintegration	Type Five

The most driving dynamism of all Enneagram types is found in the energy of Eights.

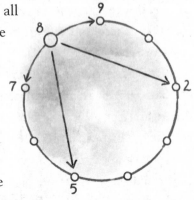

Eights are a source of strength and determination, an initiating and intimidating force of vitality in the world. A dear friend married to an Eight once told me, "They aren't as hard as they come across, but they are as mean."

As Father Richard suggested, the Eight exemplifies the fundamental need to be against. Eights are against everything. Even when they agree, they'll find a way to turn anything into combat or sparring. This is how Eights build trust—through pushing and fighting. It's their attempt to size up the trustworthiness of others, an unconscious way of determining if people will stand up to them by standing up for themselves.

You'll observe Eights being rude or offensive, trying to get a reaction out of people to see what they're made of. This behavior is partly due to their Childhood Wound, an acceleration of maturity as a result of conflict or harsh environments where they felt they needed to be strong in order to survive.

The self-survival instinct of Eights informs their Basic Fear of being destroyed—though I think more accurately it is the fear of not being in control. As children, Eights typically felt smothered, most likely by their nurturing caregiver, and so, in an effort not to be controlled by nurturing love, they rejected it and overidentified with their protective stance in the world. Ultimately this is yet another way they exert control—by *not* being controlled.

Eights are intense. Eights hate bullies but are the biggest bullies. Though Eights use their force of personality to try to convince people of their strongly held opinions, they are not so much emotional as they are impassioned. Passionate and forceful, Eights are extremists in the positions they hold, the vocations they're called to, and the causes they champion.

The traditional Passion of the Eight is lust, not necessarily sexual lust but more like a lust for intensity, which is aimed toward everything. Sometimes this lust is manifested in self-destructive behaviors, which is ironic in light of their Basic Fear.

Because Eights fear that they will be destroyed, they overdo everything to make themselves feel alive—even overdoing things that are harmful to themselves. This often leads to tremendous pain for themselves and those they love.

Eights are frequently feared in community because of the havoc they wreak. Yet the messes they make are part of how Eights grow: like a catapult for growth, the farther backward they stumble, the farther forward they fly in their revival of recovery.

Traditionally, the Fixation of the Eight is vengeance, which is first aimed at themselves. No one can be harder on Eights than themselves, and in turn Eights can be extremely hard on others—demanding more than is fair or realistic and making people pay for the ways Eights feel betrayed by them.

Eights hate to be slowed down, interrupted, or cut off.

They are intimidating and they know it, but it surprises even them because deep inside they know that they are using their strength to protect the vulnerable child within them who never seemed safe enough to grow up.

Eights with a Seven wing passionately exaggerate, overexert themselves, and excessively indulge their compulsions; they are much more cheerful and warm than Eights with a Nine wing.

With a Nine wing, an Eight is capable of holding differences in tension, balancing extremes while still being extreme, and finding ways to collaborate with diverse groups of people.

In integration Eights reach toward the Two. They levy their need to be against such things as injustice and poverty, and show up as generous and loving. Mother Teresa, with whom I spent quite a bit of time, is probably the most commonly mistyped Two. She clearly was an integrated Eight.

In disintegration Eights who can't get their way through presence and force take on the mental reductionism of the Five. They use keen insight into people to reduce them to the most easily manipulated fragment of their whole.

The Virtue of Eights is innocence, which is awakened through vulnerability. When an Eight is with a child, you see this innocence emerge—it's as if the Eight knows they can't be controlled by a little kid; they don't need to fight a child. Their propensity to assume protective roles makes them careful to look out for those who are vulnerable.

A child mirrors back to Eights what they can't see for themselves: potential and possibility stuffed behind the illusion of power, which if left unchecked is a source of pain to themselves and those around them.

TYPE NINE

Holy Idea	Holy Love
Virtue	Action
Basic Desire	Peace of mind and wholeness
Basic Fear	Loss, separation, and fragmentation
Fixation	Indolence
Passion	Sloth
Direction of Integration	Type Three
Direction of Disintegration	Type Six

Sitting at the top of the circle of the Enneagram is the Nine.

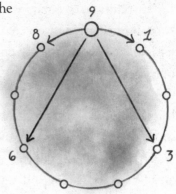

Since the Holy Idea, or the state of the mind at rest, of the Nine is Holy Love—and Saint Paul reminds us, "The greatest of these is love" (1 Corinthians 13:13)— Nines have been considered the prototype of the other archetypes within the Enneagram.

This theory is also given credence because each of the types to the left of the Nine (starting with Eight) is more "antisocial" or "rebellious," and each of the types to the right of the Nine (beginning with One) is more "social" or "seductive."[2] It's as if the Nine is the spine of a body and each of the other types are the ribs coming off that spinal cord.

As such, the Nine observes all that is and, rather than getting sucked into the drama, essentially opts out, witnessing the world without much compulsion to participate in it.

Nines withdraw in order to protect their need for autonomy. Their withdrawal may be disguised by their capacity to negotiate and mediate the lives of everyone else around them. On one hand, this keeps them from engaging their own inner life; on the other hand, they are able to lower the energy of their environment by calming everyone down and chilling everything out.

Nines commonly feel as if they lost part of themselves as children, as if others saw past or through them and failed to acknowledge them. This Childhood Wound caused them to stay under the radar and make sure everyone else was fine. Drawing attention to themselves or their needs just complicated things, so Nines detached from their needs and ensured their surroundings and loved ones were taken care of.

Attaching to love and security in relationship to their caregiver(s), Nines learned instinctively how to self-nurture and self-protect, which leads to their detached social posture. They tend to live disconnected from their bodies even though they are the Anchor Point of the Body Center. As the most disconnected of the body types, Nines seem the least angry, but the anger is there, just stuffed deep inside. There's a sort of line of violation that, once crossed, awakens Nines to their anger; it comes out suddenly, clumsy and intense, catching them and everyone else off guard. Once their anger is exposed, Nines feel guilty for feeling it and once again try to hide it from themselves by cramming it even deeper.

Nines are calm, cool, and collected. Nines are by nature understanding and make excellent arbitrators, mediators, and referees because they have an innate ability to understand almost every perspective. Because of this profound capacity to understand others, it's hard for them to take a position or hold an opinion, especially if it's contrary to that of their partner or community.

The Basic Fear of Nines is falling into the fuzzy ambiguity of their ability to empathize with multiple perspectives, ultimately losing themselves in the process and not having a place to land. Their inner stability is not to be encroached upon. As long as they feel that people are keeping their distance, Nines think they are okay. But the truth is they aren't; ultimately they need to be drawn out of themselves.

The traditional Passion of the Nine is sloth, or more accurately the lethargic, self-forgetting apathy they practice with their own drives, needs, and desires. If their external world is okay, they think they'll be okay too, thus failing to give themselves the proper self-care and attention required to wake up out of their mental and bodily inertia.

Indolence or shiftless idleness is the Nine's Fixation, a slow, simmering boil of forgetfulness that causes them to stay stuck in their own unruffled tranquility.

Nines with an Eight wing assert their instinctive ability to see through conflict with clarity and compromise in ways that feel safe and constructive.

Nines with a One wing are firmer with their conscience and principles, give more attention to details, and follow their ethical convictions into the peace they mediate.

In integration Nines engage their inner drive to bring about reconciliation in successful endeavors that bring forward true harmony.

When they lose more of themselves than they can handle, Nines slip into the disintegration path of the Six—deescalating even more than imaginable to secure peace at any cost, becoming anxious like indignant Sixes.

Ultimately the Virtue of Nines is action, manifested in proper engagement with others and a discerning restraint based in unwavering love. When Nines are present to their bodies, their own need for inner harmony, and their innate ability to project their strength into the world, no one is more capable of exemplifying the tremendous power of love to renew all things.

WHERE WE GO FROM HERE

Taking a stroll around the Enneagram circle, studying the nine types of character structure, is where many Enneagram books stop. Which is why even people who are very familiar with the Enneagram don't know what to do with it. Initially, we're so enamored with learning about ourselves that we think knowing the particularities common to our type is enough. But this knowledge is really just the beginning. And where we go from here reveals our willingness to press into our inner life, no matter how hard it may be.

6

Relationists, Pragmatists, *and* Idealists

Introducing the Harmony Triads

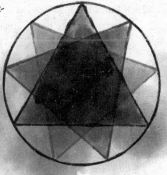

I t's not enough just to know the characteristics of each Enneagram type or even the Childhood Wound behind each type. It's critical to awaken to the wisdom brought forward through the Harmony Triads to realize and appreciate both the prayer posture and the prayer intention needed to support one's deeper development.

Understanding the head, heart, and body of the Intelligence Centers provides a good basic framework and context for grasping the structure of the nine types. But more patterns of three can be found within the Enneagram. Quite a bit has been written about some of these additional triadic sets, such as the Harmonic Groups*

---

* Often confused with the Harmony Triads developed by Dr. David Daniels, the Harmonic Groups (best explained by the Enneagram Institute) illustrate how each Enneagram type copes with obstacles in their efforts to deescalate conflict by reframing difficulties in the Positive Outlook Group made up of types Two, Seven, and Nine; attempting to understand the problem at hand in the Rational Competency Group made up of types One, Three, and Five; and reacting with impassioned intensity in the Emotional Realness Group made up of types Four, Six, and Eight.

(sometimes referred to as our type's "conflict avoidance styles") and another called the Hornevian Groups* (sometimes referred to as our type's "social styles").

These threefold groupings help us see the Enneagram as a perpetual fractal of human character structure, always replicating in patterns of three. The Intelligence Centers are the preeminent triad of the Enneagram, but these ancillary triads are illuminative in showing us additional patterns about human nature.

For our purposes here, we'll focus on just a few tripartite groups: the Intelligence Centers, the Harmony Triads, and the Dominant Affect Groups. These particular triadic groupings of Enneagram types get us beyond the surface of our type into deeper and more thrilling realms of how the Enneagram illuminates our unique path to spiritual growth.

Not to be mistaken with the Harmonic Groups, the Harmony Triads reveal what is sometimes referenced as the "hidden wholeness" tucked away in the Enneagram. "Hidden" because it assumes there are two invisible lines, one connecting types Two and Five, and another connecting types Four and Seven. "Whole" because when these two invisible lines are drawn they help create three equilateral triangles, closing that open gap at the bottom of the Enneagram (sometimes called the Existential Hole†).

---

* Don Riso and Russ Hudson built off German Neo-Freudian psychoanalyst Karen Horney's categorization of individuals' social styles based on their movement away, against, or toward others to gain what they desire as rooted in their Intelligence Center (autonomy for the instinctive or body types, affection for the heart types, and security for the head types). These social styles are Aggressive and Assertive for types Three, Seven, and Eight (demanding what they want); Detached and Withdrawn for types Four, Five, and Nine (withdrawing for what they want); and Dutiful and Compliant for types One, Two, and Six (earning what they want).

† The "Existential Hole" is part of the Enneagram's oral tradition, those mysterious bits of teaching that are passed from one student to the next. The Existential Hole is believed to be the shadowy angst, the most treacherous obstacle to overcome in integrating the heart and the head. It's shown at the bottom of the Enneagram's drawing of the irregular hexagon in the opening between types Four and Five. This hole or gap at the bottom of the Enneagram is usually where those who are dominant in type Four or Five get stuck. It's not impossible for these two types to reach across this hole to develop their wings, but it's often at the edge of the journey across this chasm that types Four and Five sometimes experience the fog of depression.

The "hidden wholeness" of the Harmony Triads is also exposed through a theory on the Intelligence Centers developed in *My Best Self: Using the Enneagram to Free the Soul* by Kathleen Hurley and Theodore Dobson. Hurley and Dobson suggest that each Enneagram type relates to all three of the Intelligence Centers by operating from a *dominant center,* by enlisting a *secondary center* they use for support, and by needing to integrate a *repressed third center.* In this case, the Harmony Triads connect each of the nine Enneagram types with the corresponding types in both their support and repressed centers, creating completed "teams" or triadic groupings that express the fullness of all three centers working accountably in relationship with one another.

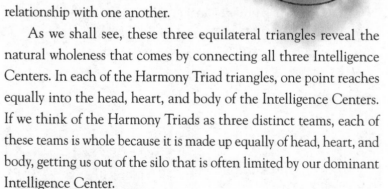

As we shall see, these three equilateral triangles reveal the natural wholeness that comes by connecting all three Intelligence Centers. In each of the Harmony Triad triangles, one point reaches equally into the head, heart, and body of the Intelligence Centers. If we think of the Harmony Triads as three distinct teams, each of these teams is whole because it is made up equally of head, heart, and body, getting us out of the silo that is often limited by our dominant Intelligence Center.

Being a head, heart, or body type isn't sufficient to support spiritual growth; we need the balance of the other two Intelligence Centers. And when we recognize where we sit in the Harmony Triad, we are ready to integrate unique contemplative prayer practices into our journey toward wholeness (a subject we will explore in detail in part 3).

Dr. David Daniels (the late clinical professor of psychiatry and behavior sciences at Stanford Medical School and a leading expert of the Enneagram in the Narrative Tradition) is credited with developing the Harmony Triads after noticing the consistent clustering of affinities the types within this triad share. Let's look more closely at what Daniels observed.

HOW THE HARMONY TRIADS
RELATE TO THE WORLD

The Harmony Triads are made up of three equilateral triangles connecting types Two, Five, and Eight (the Relationists); Three, Six, and Nine (the Pragmatists); and One, Four, and Seven (the Idealists).[1] Dr. Daniels developed these categorizations as ways the Harmony Triads *relate to the world,* in contrast to the Intelligence Centers as ways of *perceiving the world.*

This distinction is critical to understanding the Harmony Triads in relationship to the Intelligence Centers, specifically when it comes to gaining greater awareness for spiritual growth.

When joined, the three ways that the nine types perceive and translate themselves in the world (how we use our

Intelligence Center) plus the three ways the types relate to and through others in the world (how we use our Harmony Triad) create nine unique perceiving/relating combinations. These combinations further express what is exclusive to each type and also reveal the role of contemplative practice for each type.

At first it may be difficult to distinguish this carefully nuanced contrast, but think of it in terms of the difference between *perception* and *connection*. We use our Intelligence Center to *observe our connections* (how we perceive the world), while we operate out of our Harmony Triad to *connect with our observations* (how we relate to the world through our connections).

The Relationists (Twos, Fives, and Eights) "are the core exemplars of the three great moves in all relationships: toward others to meet needs and care take (type Two), away from others to deliver reason and perspective (type Five), and declarative with others, meaning to speak out and assert what is required (type Eight)."[2]

Looking at the Pragmatists (Threes, Sixes, and Nines), Daniels suggests, "Threes seek a practical and sustaining role in the world. Sixes seek to assure a

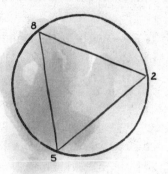

HARMONY TRIAD
RELATIONISTS

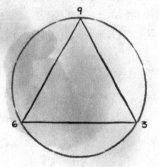

HARMONY TRIAD
PRAGMATISTS

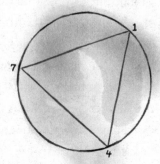

HARMONY TRIAD
IDEALISTS

safe and secure existence in the world. And Nines seek a comfortable position or place in the world."[3]

Finally, the Idealists (Ones, Fours, and Sevens) "each hold a vision of the way the world could be in order for life and spirit to thrive. Ones seek the perfect world according to the internal standards of the way things ought to be and are frustrated that this doesn't happen. Fours seek the ultimate ideal world in which nothing of importance or substance is missing and are frustrated and disappointed that this rarely happens. And Sevens seek the ideal positive world free of suffering and pain by going to something new and positive when frustration occurs."[4]

But what may be even more interesting is that each of these Harmony Triads is driven by the energy of its Heart Center type: Relationists are led by Two, Pragmatists by Three, and Idealists by Four. There's something crucial about human nature and the function of the heart.

Relationists relate to the world through connections, which is one of the dominant functions of the heart-centered Two more than any other Enneagram type. Twos make the deepest relational connections in the world.

Pragmatists relate to the world through what works and type Three brings this energy more than any other Enneagram type. Threes, rooted in the heart, are the quintessential get-it-done people, demonstrated in their litany of accomplishments.

Idealists relate to the world through their dreams for a better world. And there's no greater dreamer in the Enneagram than the Four.

I was brought up in a religious tradition that encouraged me to "ask Jesus into my heart," which reminds me of the very first time I met Mother Teresa. It was the summer of 1993, and I was in India trying to discern how to respond to my compassionate drive to fight for justice. Just twenty-one years old, I wanted to make an impression on her. A friend arranged for our introduction, and so I headed to her convent in Calcutta (the "Mother House," as they called it).

I knocked on the old wooden door and was met by a young nun from South India. The sister quietly led me to the second floor and asked that I take a seat on a concrete bench while she went to get Mother. As I sat there waiting, my mind churned with all the questions I wanted to ask Mother Teresa.

Suddenly she appeared. I immediately stood up out of respect, but she quickly took my hands and sat right beside me. Over the next thirty minutes she never let them go.

She asked about my family, where I was from, why I was in India. I realized Mother had met thousands and thousands of people, but in that moment she made me feel like she really cared about *me*. I've never known another like her. Mother's presence was simultaneously gentle and commanding, her eyes full of acceptance and love.

She needed to get back to work when I realized I never had a chance to ask all *my* questions. She was the one asking the questions instead. I could not believe it.

But as she turned to go, she had one more thing she wanted to ask. "My last question: Is Jesus in your heart?" Instantly I replied, "Yes, Mother, of course Jesus is in my heart." Apparently, I wasn't convincing. She asked again, this time with her fingers tapping my chest. "Really, I must be certain. Is Jesus in your heart, dear?" Again, I replied he was.

Mother Teresa excused herself for a moment and returned with a little yellow piece of paper. Handing it to me, she said, "Read this prayer every day and Jesus will be in your heart."

Personally, as a body type, this invitation never quite resonated with me. Maybe Mother could sense that, which is why she kept pressing the question. For head and body types, asking Jesus into your heart is a clumsy metaphor.

As Western Christians we're taught over and over again to value "the heart."

I can still hear the instructions of my childhood Sunday school teacher: "Now it's time to pray. Fold your hands, close your eyes, and bow your heads." Folding our hands gives somatic respect and reverence to one of the ways the body supports the heart above those folded hands, and bowing our head can be seen as a metaphor of submitting the mind to the heart. You may be interested to know that this Western prayer instruction is rooted in ancient Christian practice. Eastern Christianity (the Greek and Russian Orthodox traditions) also retained this practice, most notably in its spiritual classic, the *Philokalia*, where the writers repeatedly emphasize, "Put the mind in the heart."

So what is this "heart," and why does it keep coming to the forefront in spiritual formation through the centuries, including right here in the Enneagram's Harmony Triads? And what could it possibly mean for non-heart types? Why is it important?

Cynthia Bourgeault, in her recent book *The Heart of Centering Prayer: Nondual Christianity in Theory and Practice*, helps shed light on all this. In her chapter titled "The Way of the Heart" she helps us see that the "heart" as it relates to spirituality is something much more than an Enneagram Intelligence Center or the role of feelings and emotions. She writes, "In the great wisdom traditions of the West (Christian, Jewish, Islamic), the heart is first and foremost *an organ of spiritual perception*."[5] This is what the Harmony Triads are trying to express.

If the heart types of the Enneagram are anchored in their feelings and emotions, the "heart" that the Harmony Triads are exposing is the perfected "organ of spiritual perception" that is activated to relate to the world so that we can engage the world when it is brought into balance with the mind and the body.

I see this played out when my puppy Basil rolls over onto his back and exposes his heart, eager for me to connect with him by rubbing his chest. When he shows me his open chest, he is inviting me to engage him, to relate to him through touch. Basil only risks exposing the most vulnerable part of himself when he knows he is safe and loved. The same is true for us.

The problem is that we don't know we're safe and loved. The Enneagram helps us get to the root of this insecurity so that we can reconnect with the safety and love that is God.

To open the "heart" of every type is an invitation to live life to the fullest. To live in a world that needs to be engaged through harmonious love. And the Enneagram, as seen through the Harmony Triads, coupled with contemplative practice, helps us do just that—no matter what our Intelligence Center is.

DOMINANT AFFECT GROUPS

The Enneagram Institute calls the groupings of the Harmony Triads the "Dominant Affect Groups." It's a different way of looking at the same thing. If the Harmony Triads help us understand how we relate to the world as either Relationists, Pragmatists, or Idealists, the Dominant Affect Groups offer the clarifying layer of how each of the triads is informed by a person's early defining relationships and how this, in turn, forms each type's psychosocial development. When we view the Harmony Triads and Dominant Affect Groups together, we begin to grasp the dynamic prism of our spiritual development.

I'm convinced the Enneagram Institute's material on this specific triad is one of the most underappreciated discoveries of the modern Enneagram. And with the understanding of the Enneagram evolving so rapidly, there's no better time than now to press deeper into this material.

You may remember *object relations theory* from an introduction to psychology course or from that first time you reclined on a therapist's couch and were asked about your mother. Object relations has to do with how our identity developed through the mirroring action of our caregiver(s) in the first few years of life. It is often explained through an infant's initial ten-inch depth of vision, essentially the distance between their eyes and the eyes of their nursing parent—typically the first "object" in a baby's experience. This first object, the source of nurturance for children who are breastfed, supports the psychodynamic theory that our psyche emerges in relationship to the protective and/or nurturing* objects that aid in the development of our consciousness.

So if the Harmony Triads tell us about *how we relate to the world*, the Dominant Affect Groups go a step further by telling us how we relate to the world *specifically* as a result of

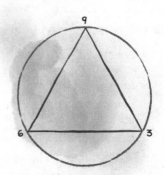

DOMINANT AFFECT GROUP
REJECTION TYPES

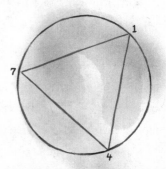

DOMINANT AFFECT GROUP
ATTACHMENT TYPES

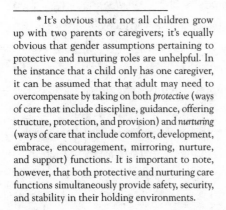

DOMINANT AFFECT GROUP
FRUSTRATION TYPES

---

* It's obvious that not all children grow up with two parents or caregivers; it's equally obvious that gender assumptions pertaining to protective and nurturing roles are unhelpful. In the instance that a child only has one caregiver, it can be assumed that that adult may need to overcompensate by taking on both *protective* (ways of care that include discipline, guidance, offering structure, protection, and provision) and *nurturing* (ways of care that include comfort, development, embrace, encouragement, mirroring, nurture, and support) functions. It is important to note, however, that both protective and nurturing care functions simultaneously provide safety, security, and stability in their holding environments.

our defining family relationships—what drives the Harmony Triads or the *why* behind the Harmony Triads.

Understanding this interconnection helps move us past simple observations about character structure and gets us to the ways our relationship with our caregivers served as a confirmation bias in strengthening our attachment to our type. It can open our eyes to some of the reasons behind why we think, act, and feel as we do.

When the Enneagram Institute applies object relations theory as it relates to our childhood caregivers, it's often explained like this:

Rejection Types	
Type Two	Felt rejected because the nurturing love they offered their protective caregiver wasn't reciprocated, so overidentifies with nurturing energy.
Type Five	Rejected both the nurturing and protective caregivers as intrusive and withdrew to assume a self-nurturing and self-protective stance.
Type Eight	Felt controlled by the nurturing love they were offered by their caregiver and rejected it, so overidentifies with protective energy.
Attachment Types	
Type Three	Attaches to the energy of the nurturing caregiver and subsequently becomes capable of self-nurturing.
Type Six	Attaches to the energy of the protective caregiver and subsequently becomes capable of self-protection.
Type Nine	Attaches to the energy of both the nurturing and protective caregivers and subsequently becomes capable of self-nurturing and self-protection.
Frustration Types	
Type One	Is frustrated the protective caregiver didn't safeguard enough, so compensates by assuming a self-protective stance.
Type Four	Is frustrated the nurturing and protective caregivers didn't offer enough, so compensates by assuming self-protection and self-nurture.
Type Seven	Is frustrated the nurturing caregiver didn't nurture enough, so compensates by assuming a self-nurturing stance.

In the Dominant Affect Groups, the three equilateral Harmony Triad triangles form these object relations collections: Two, Five, and Eight (the Rejection Group); Three, Six, and Nine (the Attachment Group); and One, Four, and Seven (the Frustration Group).[6]

The Rejection Group (or the Harmony Triads' Relationists) mirrors the Dominant Affect Groups of the Harmony Triads with the Twos, Fives, and Eights. The rejection this group experienced causes these types to deflect their needs by rejecting what they want.

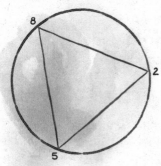

HARMONY TRIAD RELATIONISTS

DOMINANT AFFECT GROUP REJECTION TYPES

Riso and Hudson observe, "These types go through life expecting to be rejected and so they defend themselves against this feeling. . . . They repress their own genuine needs and vulnerabilities."[7]

The Rejection Group uses emotional stiff-arm techniques to push away what they don't want to be controlled by, while simultaneously pulling toward themselves the kind of love they can't give themselves. It's suggested that their rejection was confused in their early developmental years by shutting down what they felt they needed so they'd not be prone to attach to it or feel frustrated by it.

Twos simply want to be loved for who they are, but they are fearful their needs will be too demanding and lead to rejection, so they repress their own needs by focusing on meeting the needs of others. Relational security (the prevention of rejection) means having as few needs as possible, so Fives resist exposing their needs by protecting themselves with emotional distance. Because of their fear of being controlled, Eights refuse to open their hearts and reject the possibility of needing anyone else. Eights also resist facing their pain and would rather fight for those in poverty or those who suffer in pain than press into their own. This proximity to vulnerability and pain is one of the ways they are confronted by their inability to be vulnerable themselves, not allowing themselves to want or ask or need for anything or anyone.

Twos felt rejected when their protective caregiver couldn't reciprocate love in the nurturing manner they desired, which caused them to become overly nurturing. Fives felt intruded upon by both their protective and nurturing caregivers and retreated to self-nurture and self-protection. Eights rejected the loving attempts of care from their nurturing caregiver, fearful they'd be controlled by it, and subsequently became overly protective.[8]

Essentially these three types reject what they most want in relationships. These types must learn to be truthful about their needs; their willingness to have their needs met is the first step in their spiritual journey home.

The Attachment Group (or the Harmony Triads' Pragmatists) is made up of the Anchor Points (or midpoints) of the Intelligence Centers; this group takes hold of the practical energies they find that support their own sense of self.

Riso and Hudson put it this way: "*Attachment* represents the desire of the ego to maintain a comfortable and stable relationship with people or things that [those in the Attachment group] are identified with . . . [they] want to hold on to whatever works."[9]

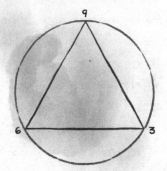

HARMONY TRIAD
PRAGMATISTS

DOMINANT AFFECT GROUP
ATTACHMENT TYPES

Simply put, the Attachment Group scaffolds their inner insecurities

in relationship to their needs for recognition (Threes), stability (Sixes), or independence (Nines), and fastens either their feelings, instincts, or thoughts (their Intelligence Center) to these.

Threes attach to the positions that draw attention back to their empty hearts; Sixes attach to external forces that reassure them of who they are in their minds; Nines attach to exterior distractions to avoid having to wake up in their bodies and move inward with honesty.

Their attachment is a reflection of their relationship with their caregivers at an early age, when a deep hunger to feed their attachment was met (with recognition, stability, or independence) by either their nurturing caregiver, their protective caregiver, or both.

The affection the Three gives or receives from their *nurturing* caregiver fuels their natural ability to self-nurture; the Six's sense of safety with their *protective* caregiver sustains their innate ability to maintain an inner protective state; and the Nine's instinctive craving to attach to both their *nurturing* and *protective* caregivers fortifies the self-nurturing and self-protective posture they withdraw to.[10]

Essentially, these three types attach to what works for them *pragmatically*. Knowing this helps them recognize that they need to engage practical ways of nurturing their spirituality in prayer.

The Frustration Group (the Harmony Triads' Idealists), made up of Ones, Fours, and Sevens, experience constant angst about what could be. As little children they were frustrated they weren't given enough of what they sensed they needed to self-realize.

Riso and Hudson suggest, "*Frustration* relates to our feelings

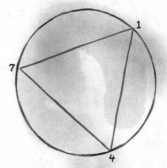

HARMONY TRIAD
IDEALISTS

DOMINANT AFFECT GROUP
FRUSTRATION TYPES

that our comfort and needs are not being sufficiently attended to. . . . None of these types ever seems to be able to find what it is looking for."[11]

The Frustration Group plays out their persistent irritation through unrealistic expectations for themselves and others (Ones), intense introspection in their quest for authenticity in themselves and the world (Fours), and the fear that bringing closure to an experience or an idea ultimately limits their freedom (Sevens).

The Frustration Group scaffolds their inner insecurities in relationship to their needs for autonomy (Ones), validation and recognition (Fours), or access to opportunity (Sevens), and fastens their feelings, instincts, or thoughts to these.

Their frustration was also realized in relationship with their caregivers at an early age when they experienced a compulsion for more care or safety from either their nurturing caregiver, their protective caregiver, or both. They just wanted more than they seemed to be receiving and that frustration never left.

The One's disapproval of their protective caregiver's imperfections propelled them to take on a protective stance. The Four's insatiable need for affectionate attention from their nurturing and protective caregivers fueled their turning inward for self-nurture and self-protection. And the Seven's ravenous need to consume caring love prompted them to constantly nurture their own needs as a way of avoiding their pain.[12]

Fundamentally these three types are constantly frustrated by their own idealism. Growing in awareness helps them recognize their desperate need to rest in God, discovering wholeness through prayer.

FOCUSING THE LENS OF TYPE
THROUGH TRIADS

Understanding the Harmony Triads gives clarity when attempting to find ways to ground ourselves within our Intelligence Centers.

If the Intelligence Centers are our *primary modes of perceiving the world* and the Harmony Triads are *the ways we relate to the world*, then merging the centers with these specific triads offers nine unique combinations that explain how we *translate* our perceptions of our relationship with being:

Type One	The Instinctive Frustrated Idealist
Type Two	The Emotionally Rejecting Relationist
Type Three	The Emotionally Attached Pragmatist
Type Four	The Emotionally Frustrated Idealist
Type Five	The Rational Rejecting Relationist
Type Six	The Rationally Attached Pragmatist
Type Seven	The Rational Frustrated Idealist
Type Eight	The Instinctive Rejecting Relationist
Type Nine	The Instinctive Attached Pragmatist

So our Intelligence Centers illuminate how we *see* the world, and our Harmony Triads illuminate how we *relate* to and engage the world. Both provide penetrating self-awareness that helps dismantle the illusions of personality or the False Self, thereby exposing how we see and engage God.

We will see that adopting a Harmony Triad-specific contemplative prayer intention is what we most need to facilitate wholeness. Our specific *prayer intention*—the inner disposition we bring to support our contemplative *prayer posture*—helps us wake up from the slumber of illusions around our identity and relationships. Waking up is the first step in the spiritual journey, a courageous alternative to the fantasies we fashion to keep us asleep.

Aligning contemplative prayer postures of solitude, silence, and stillness with our Intelligence Centers and associating contemplative prayer intentions of consent, engagement, and rest with our Harmony Triads just might be the most effective way to start realizing the truth about who we really are. And when we're truthful with ourselves, like young Dorothy stuck in Oz, we wake up and discover the way home.

This overlay—the resonance between these centers and triads—points beyond the limiting paradigms of personality and liberates our True Self to flourish.

But much like the Yellow Brick Road that Dorothy must travel, this journey is a long and arduous pilgrimage that requires a commitment, not necessarily to the *destination*, but more specifically to the *quest* itself. The sacred map offered by the Enneagram dignifies the journey. Giving ourselves to this path requires a disciplined cultivation of spiritual depth accessible only through faithful contemplative practice that brings us into the transforming presence of a loving God.

PART

III

FINDING *Your* UNIQUE PATH *to* SPIRITUAL GROWTH

7

The Unexpected Gifts *of* Solitude, Silence, *and* Stillness

Returning to Our True Identity through
Contemplative Practice

I used to be afraid of silence.

Yet all the ancient mystics understood that silence is vital to bringing the fragmented parts of self into a vibrant whole. The sixteenth-century Spanish mystic St. John of the Cross wrote, "Silence is God's first language." Slowly I've learned to appreciate its value to my own healing and growth. But it wasn't that way in the beginning.

My first spiritual director, the late Bob Ginn, would welcome me into a little room in the back of a religious bookstore in downtown Omaha where we'd meet each month for an hour of sacred listening. Our meetings would always begin with a pause, intentional space for silence. It used to make me mad, his stubborn insistence that I practice silence; after all, I thought I was going to *talk* to him about my spiritual struggles. Guess the joke was on me since clearly my soul struggle was in consenting to contemplative practice.

As a younger man, Bob was a successful lawyer on the rise, but his career had ended after an accident in which he sustained quadriplegic injuries. Eventually, his wheelchair became for him a sort of monastery that forced him to go inward. Years after his accident, Bob cultivated a profound spirituality few souls experience.[1]

And so, when we met, Bob would invite me to share silence with him. Sometimes the silence lasted just a few moments; other times it seemed as if most of the hour was spent without words.

I think he knew it was hard for me. In fact, sometimes it was downright agonizing. I often felt extremely uncomfortable. But those quiet moments were just what I needed. The silence invited me to consider ways of praying that were new to me—prayer that required my full self, my whole person in the presence of God, yet prayer that didn't always use words.

And if I'm honest, I'm still sometimes afraid of silence.

In silence, I'm unable to control my environment.

In silence, I'm forced to face myself, allowing all my fears, shame, guilt, regrets, disappointments, doubts, and resentments to come to the surface.

In silence, my ambition and drive slow down just enough for my mind to come up with new thoughts, unwanted (though sometimes important) to-do lists, and more ideas than I know what to do with.

Sometimes silence is downright exhausting. It's an assault on my mind and emotions, not the imagined blissful experience I wish it would be. In other words, silence is usually a huge workout for my soul.

But with practice come moments of breaking through the internal chaos. I experience the grace of letting go—of my insecurities about not being in control, of my pains and discomforts, of even the new, intriguing thoughts churning through my mind. And then, I find love.

Love from God.

Love for God.

Love from myself.

Love for myself.

Love from others.

Love for others.

As an extrovert, I somehow find silence easier to engage when I'm surrounded by others. That might sound ridiculous, but I'm not alone in this. The nonprofit I now run with Phileena hosts a weekly public contemplative prayer sit every Wednesday at 4:00 p.m. (our UPS delivery guy used to think we were conducting a sleep study), and some of the people who gather spend more time driving to the prayer sit than they spend at the sit itself. The opportunity to meditate in a supportive community is worth the journey.

I'm always surprised at who shows up. Surprised that so many people would go out of their way to stop. To pause. To rest their minds and open their hearts.

What's even more surprising is the small community that has formed around these relatively short moments of silence. It's always an eclectic group that gathers—people of all faiths and no faith—yet each participant clearly cares deeply about their spirituality. All of them value the mysteries realized only in silence.

They come. They gather. Quietly. Undramatically. Some enter in silence and leave in silence; some utter barely more than a polite greeting and brief word of parting. As a gesture of reverence, a few folks take off their shoes outside the door, discreetly slipping them back on as they leave.

A young mother joined us the first couple of years, bringing her two- and four-year-old daughters who seemed to be better at silence than the rest of us. Astonishingly, those two little girls sat perfectly still and quiet for the entire twenty minutes. We'd always "reward" them by passing around a small bowl with dark chocolate and sea salt caramels after our silent session was over—a tradition we hold to this day (even when no children are part of the circle).

There are quite a few regulars, but each week we always have at least one or two newcomers. Everyone is welcome, including our puppy Basil. He has his own orange prayer mat that he silently curls up on.

Frequently you will find a very traditional Catholic priest sitting across from an Episcopal bishop, or perhaps it's a conservative preacher from the Southern Baptist suburban megachurch seated beside a progressive theologian from the nearby Jesuit university. Those who normally would be divided by doctrine and belief come together in unity. Through their words they would find plenty about which to disagree, but silence brings them into a new kind of communion, forming a new kind of community.

I have spent most of my life bringing people together around ideas, causes, events, meals, social justice initiatives, and other meaningful opportunities. It has been a value of mine to nurture extremely diverse groups of conversation partners, forming all kinds of seemingly incompatible communities and unlikely social circles.

But the group that meets on Wednesdays is special. What is it about silence that allows uncommon people to find common ground?

When I come out of the sit, the love I've tapped into allows me to breathe more deeply and more slowly, my eyes to move across the room more gently, and my words to be fewer. When I come out of silence in our community prayer sits, everyone around me looks a little more beautiful, perhaps a wee bit angelic.

My sense is that the mystery of silence draws us deeper into love, and love is something that we cannot control; love invites us into fresh ways of thinking and unfamiliar ways of being.

Fundamentally, love is at the heart of our Christian faith tradition. God *is* love, and in consenting to silence, we allow Love to wash over us, inviting us into a "new we," a new kind of community that affirms the divine imprint within all humanity and contributes to building the kind of world we all want to live in.

In silence, we experience the gentleness of love despite all our attempts to resist it.

In silence, we discover a transcendent union of body, mind, soul, and spirit—the integration of our whole selves.

In silence, our union with God and within ourselves allows for surprising unity with others. Indeed, unity in silence has become an unexpected gift.

In silence, the fragmented parts of self come into greater wholeness. And over time, we experience, through silence, the wisdom of the Enneagram—a gentle invitation to come home to our True Self.

It's not enough to just become an Enneagram enthusiast. Real transformation takes place when we pair the self-awareness that the Enneagram stimulates with the silence of contemplative practice. Then our unique path to spiritual growth emerges, and we will never be the same.

In silence, the gifts of our identity begin to emerge—this is one of the hallmark fruits of contemplative practice. Of course, we have to fight for it.

THE BEST WAY OUT IS THROUGH

To understand the Enneagram in its modern Western form and use, we have to remember that it was originally (and quietly) brought to the States by a South American psychiatrist (Claudio Naranjo) and then unleashed by a spiritual community (the Jesuits). With this context, it's no surprise the Enneagram is largely framed as a tool for psychology and spirituality.

As an attempt to offer some guidance to this approach, let me suggest that the Enneagram offers practical and specific paths to spiritual formation that are unique to each type.

Essentially, the Enneagram teaches us how to be more human.

It is one of the most profound tools for personal and spiritual transformation. And to make the most of its offerings, we are invited to move beyond identifying our type toward putting this knowledge to work—to form a new identity, or perhaps more accurately, to reclaim our original identity. The Enneagram helps us find our unique path to spiritual growth, and this path is ultimately how we find our way home.

Though finding our way home may seem an exciting prospect at the outset, the ego continually resists attempts to wake up and move from illusion to truth. The tendency of the ego is to remain in its smug and content cave of unawareness, convincing itself of the illusion of personality. Fundamentally, the ego must undergo a series of conversions that lead to truth, but each of these conversions is simultaneously a small death of the ego that is viciously resisted by the defense mechanisms of our Enneagram types.

This, I believe, is the true nature of conversion: it happens not in a single moment or pivotal event but in a lifelong series of minor deaths. It is what Jesus spoke plainly of: "If you wish to come after me, you must deny your very selves, take up the instrument of your own death and follow in my footsteps" (Matthew 16:24).

These small deaths are painful. They seem overwhelming. Most of us are too scared to face them. But just as when the Scarecrow reminded Dorothy and their fellow traveling companions before entering the haunted forest, "It'll get darker before it gets lighter," so is the nature of inner work.

In his beautiful poem "A Servant to Servants," Robert Frost suggests that "the best way out is always through," and this wisdom is especially apt in connection with the Enneagram. The best way out of our deceptive self-illusion is through hard inner work. As we work with the Enneagram, we can't avoid pressing through our ego's set of coping addictions. We can't help but face the ways we've kept ourselves asleep in our illusions. Waking up means telling ourselves the truth about those subconscious techniques fortifying the scaffolding around the lies we believe about our own ego mythologies. The Enneagram won't let us sidestep the interior work of separating the truth from the lies we've told ourselves over and over and over again.

The Enneagram forces us to wake up out of our illusion-of-self and break free from the shackles of our personality. Once we awaken, we can no longer continue to live in the dreamlike states of the deceptions that we have convinced ourselves are more real and more dramatic than the best of who we can become when freed from the prisons of our Fixations and Passions.

Not only do we have to traverse through the chaos and darkness of our fragmented identity, but we also have to die to who we thought we were. And nothing helps us embrace the death of our personality structure more than contemplative practice. Make no mistake, contemplative prayer does feel like death because it's a way to practice how to die. It's a one-way pilgrimage, a lot like Dorothy's quest to find her way home in *The Wizard of Oz*, once she realizes she can't get back to Kansas the way she came. And we know pilgrimages don't end; they merely facilitate new beginnings. This new way of finding our way home is the first of a series of minor deaths to which we must submit. And it can be scary.

A dear friend, Pastor Drew Jackson, spent the last days of his mother's life accompanying her through her death, a painful and heart-wrenching journey for them both. Not long after, we spent a weekend together on a retreat hosted by my nonprofit. There Drew shared one of the most profound thoughts on the contemplative journey I've ever heard.

Life best lived is lived as a series of losses, a series of deaths. Death is not meant to be a one-time event at the end of life but, rather, a daily experience by which we learn to continually embrace the unknown, step into mystery, and release the need to control. . . . The contemplative way is a practice in "death." If you have ever witnessed the moment of death, you know that death is ultimately silent, still, and alone. The practices of contemplative spirituality prepare us for this. The contemplative way thrusts us into the beautiful struggle of embracing the unknown and losing the need to control.[2]

This is hard . . . it seems almost impossible. But Love, found in the silence, carries us through the agony of loss. Love returns us to the possibilities of life. As the prayer of Saint Francis reminds us, "It is in dying that we are born into eternal life."

Drew went on to say, "As we learn to practice death by way of contemplation, death at the end of life is no longer a fear, but is received as the next logical step. Death is no longer an unknown for us because we already know that life comes through the process of death. We will have lived that reality each day."[3]

There's no better way to live into our new life or original essence than with the help of contemplative practice. But we resist dying. It doesn't come easy for us. Everything in us fights to hold on to what we think is life. We see this in how the Enneagram's Passions—the sincere yet misguided ways we attempt to return to our True Self—try to help us feel alive even though in their addictive form they lead to self-destruction.

To step into the life that is truly life, we're invited to practice for our death. But voluntarily preparing to die seems counterintuitive, and contemplative prayer hardly seems the obvious first step on this journey. What's so difficult here is how undramatic the process is for such a dramatic hoped-for result. But as author Eckhart Tolle writes, "True happiness is found in seemingly unremarkable things. But to be aware of little, quiet things, you need to be quiet inside. A high degree of alertness is required. Be still. Look. Listen. Be present."[4]

That is the essence of contemplative practice. And that is where our transformation is activated.

WHAT IS CONTEMPLATIVE SPIRITUALITY?

In her book *Pilgrimage of a Soul*, Phileena says that contemplative spirituality carves the posture of surrender (letting go) into the fabric of our being, making us receptive to transformation. She goes on: "Contemplative spirituality is a state of being. It's the portal to the direct life-giving presence of God. When rooted in contemplative spirituality we are more receptive and supple in the hands of God; the life of Christ flows more freely through us."[5]

Solitude, silence, and stillness are the quintessential qualities of contemplative prayer and practice. Phileena writes, "By abandoning ourselves regularly to God through prayer in the form of solitude, silence and stillness, we experience more freedom *from* compulsions and heavy-laden expectations and more liberty *in* our [T]rue [S]elf with all of our unique gifts to offer the world."[6]

Solitude, silence, and stillness are the corrections to the compulsions that come out of our Intelligence Centers, our head, heart, and gut. Together they make us whole. They bring us home.

True contemplatives aren't superspiritual elites or those committed ascetics who completely withdraw from the world. True contemplatives don't simply nurture their inner life in isolation. Contemplative spirituality is critical for everyone. Especially in an age when we are constantly interrupted by digital distractions, contemplation invites us to return to the present moment where God can be encountered.

The true contemplative is any normal person who allows deep soul work to lead to a broad, outward-facing transformation. That's the beauty of contemplative practice: we enter it as individuals, yet emerge enriched and equipped, part of a larger community more capable of serving the needs of a hurting world. Likewise, true activists do not simply throw themselves at a cause for the sake of the cause without first allowing a passion or focus to provide some sort of anchor or grounding point. And so, bringing contemplation and activism together creates a fresh kind of accountability to both efforts, illuminating for us the truth that neither can be isolated from the other if we really want to have an impact.

Mother Teresa was an outstanding example of the blending of contemplation and activism. During my time living in India, I frequently visited her and the community she led in Calcutta. Every moment I shared with her was life-changing. The simple words she spoke were credible because of the life she lived. And Mother Teresa lived a very active life; she was very present to real human needs. But five times a day, every day, she would stop for prayer. She would stop for mass. She would take time for silence. These were quiet, undramatic, mundane moments that neither received news coverage nor drew much attention. Yet I believe that without these intentional pauses, her impact on the world never would have had the scope it did.

I used to think that Mother's fecundity needed to be supported by her prayer life, but as I watched her simple commitment to nurturing her own spirituality, it dawned on me that she didn't pray to support her work, but in fact *the work was the fruit of her prayers.* She led with contemplative prayer, and goodness came forward.

How did she do it? She took consistent sacred pauses to nurture an inner solitude, silence, and stillness.

Today when I talk about contemplative spirituality, I'm referring to a faith rooted in practices marked by postures of solitude, silence, and stillness, which may seem similar yet are distinct ways of encountering God with our whole presence and person. Solitude, silence, and stillness are the lifesaving corrections to the absurdity we've fallen into—the addictions or whatever is out of control in our lives. Adopting contemplative practice is crucial to living into the transformation and wholeness reflected in the Enneagram.

Solitude

Lots of us are surrounded by people all the time. Many of the people we know, many of the people with whom we interact, and many of the groups we work with are community-oriented, community-based, community-focused. Many of our friends have multiple roommates. Many can't go to the grocery store alone. Even when we aren't physically present with each other, our days are punctuated with texts, tweets, and social media interactions. But somehow people still feel deeply and profoundly lonely.

Solitude, intentional withdrawal, teaches us to be present—present to ourselves, present to God, and present with others.

Silence

We're constantly distracted, forever listening to a subtext that keeps us from focusing. There is so much noise in our lives—emails, texts, phone calls, Twitter notifications, Instagram notifications, Facebook updates—that we are unable to hear, to listen. Our attention is always being interrupted.

Silence actually teaches us to listen. It helps us learn how to listen to the voice of God, a voice we maybe have not been able to recognize. It helps us listen to the people in our lives who speak loving, truthful words of correction or affirmation to us. In silence we hear the truth that God is not as hard on us as we are on ourselves.

Stillness

We live in a cause-driven age. Our neighborhoods are filled with activists, people who care about getting behind the things that they believe will help build a better world. Efforts to establish peace and justice have become part of our social fabric. Just look at people's social media accounts to see how they've branded themselves around their humanitarian concerns. It seems all of us want to do good in the world; we want to help. But in many ways the world is getting worse, not better, despite our best intentions.

In addition to our drive to build a better world, we also live in a time when productivity and impact feed the lies we believe about ourselves. The constant pressure to do more, to fill up our schedules, to work harder. But we have to stop the busyness or we will be stopped by burnout and exhaustion.

Stillness teaches us restraint, and in restraint we are able to discern what appropriate engagement looks like.

Giving ourselves to solitude, silence, and stillness not only nurtures the inner spirituality our souls long for but also quiets the mind in a way that offers us the chance to make major corrections to our behaviors that are otherwise obscured by life's noises. It helps us reconnect with God through deep and focused communion. It helps us face the series of minor deaths required in our pilgrimages home.

Solitude, silence, and stillness lead to better holistic health, with benefits for the mind, soul, and body. We walk slower, we lift our heads a little higher, and we see things we haven't seen before.

The contemplative lifestyle reveals its power by way of the fruit it produces. Contemplative practices and disciplines affect every part of us and our relationships. As my wife Phileena always says, "To the extent we are transformed, the world is transformed."

WHY CONTEMPLATION?

In all of his winsome wisdom, Cistercian monk Father Thomas Keating writes:

> This is the human condition—to be without the true source of happiness which is the experience of the presence of God, and to have lost the key to happiness which is the contemplative dimension of life, the path to the increasing assimilation and enjoyment of God's presence. What we experience is our desperate search for happiness where it cannot be found . . . [the key] was not lost outside ourselves. It was lost inside ourselves. This is where we need to look for it.[7]

This is Dorothy's revelation at the end of *The Wizard of Oz*, when the good witch Glinda reminds her, "You've always had the power to go back to Kansas." And Dorothy, who has known this intuitively, replies, "If I ever go looking for my heart's desire again I won't look any further than my own backyard. Because if it isn't there, I never really lost it to begin with."

Most of us who start down the contemplative path of spiritual formation quickly realize that we will always be beginners. There's tremendous grace in this realization because so many of us find the contemplative tradition intimidating. It seems so much more complicated, with such a steeper learning curve, than some of the other ways we've learned to "do" our inner work. (Indeed, we may lament the ways our faith communities have failed to adequately prepare us for the challenge.)

But that's okay.

Western society is on the front side of a major renewal in prioritizing and finding value in contemplative practice. For example, we see mindfulness, meditation, and yoga showing up everywhere—mindfulness at technology conferences, meditation in public schools, and even yoga in prisons. Do a quick internet search and you'll see articles about contemplative practice showing up throughout popular media. What the rest of the world is discovering is that mindfulness connects us with our head, meditation opens our hearts, and yoga reconnects us with our bodies.

Sadly, with few exceptions, Christianity has resisted a return to its historic contemplative tradition and thus has lost an opportunity to lead beyond the worn-out culture wars we often seem to return to.

But I have hope that Christianity will return to its contemplative roots. We see the rumblings of this return in what our friend, the late Phyllis Tickle (one of the great American religion writers of our time), called Christianity's "rummage sales," or what the American missiologist Ralph Winters called Christianity's "supercenturies"—those times when we reexamine and refresh our expression of what real faith looks like in the real world.

I first came across this idea in my friend Scott Bessenecker's book *The New Friars*.[8] Scott writes about Dr. Winters's research (originally sourced from Kenneth Scott Latourette's *A History of Christianity*) that organized the first two thousand years of Christianity into supercenturies that occur once every four hundred years: centuries that facilitated renewal or growth, a sort of "soft reset."

- The Classical Renaissance around AD 400
- The Carolingian Renaissance around AD 800
- The Medieval Renaissance around AD 1200
- The Reformation and Counter-Reformation around AD 1600

Phyllis Tickle's take on this is that Christianity has these "rummage sales" to essentially "clean out its attic" every five hundred years, again a sort of reset that creates an environment for newness. Tickle observes these as follows:

- The fall of the Roman Empire or the start of the Dark Ages in the sixth century
- The Great Schism of the eleventh century
- The Great Reformation of the sixteenth century[9]

So here we are, at the outset of AD 2000—the twenty-first century—potentially on the front side of what may be the next great rummage sale or supercentury of Christianity. Scott suggests that it might be the so-called New Monastic or New Friar movement leading us back to a return of intentional, missional communities much like the traditional monastic and friar communities. Phyllis Tickle suggested it may be a "Great Emergence" that redefines Christianity, a renewal whose birth pains may have been expressed in the so-called emerging/emergent church movement.

It seems to me this possible renewal is a return to a Christianity deeply rooted in its contemplative tradition, a return that is increasingly becoming attractive and accessible to everyone no matter their starting point. In our digital age, contemplative practice is not only wildly subversive but wildly life-giving—a counter to the noise and frenzy that dominate our lives.

For me, it was an unexpected introduction by my late spiritual director, Bob Ginn, in the summer of 2002 that made me realize my own faith formation had been painfully distant from any contemplative focus.

One morning I woke up to an assertive yet gentle voicemail from Bob. He apologized for not thinking of it sooner but asked if Phileena and I could join him that afternoon for lunch. He was hosting a very special guest whom he wanted us to meet.

That special guest turned out to be Thomas Keating. We thought we were familiar with most of the historic Christian contemplative prayer practices, but Father Thomas's teaching resonated deeply with who we were and where we were at that point in our lives.

That lunch changed everything.

As we sat with one of modern Christianity's greatest mystics, we were captivated by his compassionate strength. We hung on Father Thomas's every word, astonished by the embodied credibility of his message. As with any great teacher or mentor, we learned more from watching his example than from merely listening to his words. The fruit of his prayer life was awe-inspiring. I've rarely experienced anything like that first introduction to Father Thomas. Though we had been introduced to Centering Prayer by our spiritual directors, that day we learned more than just a meditation technique; we were exposed to a lifestyle of consent, engagement, and rest.

As we began to nurture a contemplative posture in our prayer lives, we became attuned to the many different methods we had unsuccessfully used to try to sustain our vocations. Responding to a call into service is important, we realized, but we became especially interested in the ways that people move from merely *sustaining* their work to *thriving* in their areas of service. Certainly, our twenty-plus years of humanitarian work sprang out of love and devotion to God, but often our work was a poor attempt to serve or please God rather than to display the natural fruit of God's love in us. Centering Prayer turned this upside down. This ancient way of praying seemed like a powerful way of supporting a very demanding vocation drenched in the needs of the world.

And so, for several years we quietly practiced old ways of praying that still felt new to us. But I'd be lying if I said Centering Prayer is easy, because it truly is one of the most difficult disciplines I've ever tried to cultivate. As many times as I tried, I gave up, only to find myself desperately bumping around the bottom of my life, experiencing some of my most tragic personal failures. And that surprised me. How could I have seen such tremendous growth in my inner life only to turn around and fall flat on my face?

But that's the fruit of the contemplative life—it helps empty out the junk that we stuff into the storehouses we call our souls. Sometimes harsh scraping is required to loosen and remove the toxic mental clutter and debris.

As I was forced to be honest about all the soul rubbish I was clinging to, I began what was the most significant transition in my life. I was about to make an unplanned and unexpected vocational passage that I now know was inevitable. I had been part of an international humanitarian organization for twenty years. It was the work I had done since graduating from university, and the community I had helped build had become a kind of family to me.

My coworkers and I had dedicated our lives to building a better world by combating human trafficking, caring for children impacted by the global AIDS pandemic, and opening drop-in centers and community centers for youth who lived, worked, and slept on the streets. The work had taken me all over the world and provided deep meaning for my sense of self and my notions of who I was.

Having struggled with my own tragic flaws for a few years, I knew it was time to move on. And looking back on those decades of service, I was finally able to admit to myself that though I had given my best and done my best, there were blind spots that held me back.

These painful moments of clarity came in the quietness of spiritual practice when I was no longer distracting myself from the harmful lies I had come to believe about my identity. When I actually took time to stop—ceasing the fight for justice, which was frequently a proxy war for the inner work I was refusing to focus on—I finally began to learn to be present, to listen, and to practice much-needed restraint.

Confronting the mirror of True Self-awareness was painful. But this honesty was the only thing, I'm convinced, that was able to usher me into healing.

First, like many people in social justice–driven vocations, I was often guilty of doing a much better job taking care of others than caring for myself. Somehow I thought it was my Christian duty to sacrifice my own needs, even my own well-being, in order to serve others better. As you can imagine, this fueled a harmful martyr mentality that I would often rub some Bible on to justify. But I don't believe God is ever honored by our burnout, even on behalf of the worthiest of efforts.

In the end, the overexertion caught up with me. Neglecting my own spiritual, emotional, and psychological needs left me empty, and in that emptiness I turned to addictive behaviors that only kept me feeling more trapped. Those harmful choices were a pitiful substitution for real self-care, clearly just coping strategies to avoid facing the truth. There's no integrity in this approach to service. The Scriptures tell us, "Love your neighbor as yourself," but most of us never really learn to love ourselves, thinking we can make up for this deficit if we practice loving others. We have to practice what love is by making room for who we are—the good and the bad. Otherwise, the love we offer others will always lack the depth of its potential.

Second, like many people in the field of social justice, I would go hard and intense—driving new ideas, recruiting amazing talent, and promoting the work through a robust speaking schedule—but the fast pace was wearing me down. I was tired. Always tired. I eventually found myself living from retreat to retreat or from vacation to vacation.

Since then I've done my best to protect rhythms that are healthy and sustainable. Today I know that Sabbath is for *rest*, retreats are for *reflection*, vacations are for *recreation*, and sabbatical is for *renewal*.

But in those days, there was never a true Sabbath. Just getting to a retreat or vacation felt like an exhausted marathon runner using the weight of their body to tear a thin finish line ribbon. And in twenty years I took just one true sabbatical, which was actually an abbreviated version of what I should have taken. When we don't honor our rhythms and neglect caring for ourselves, then the luxury of sabbatical ends up being wasted on *recovery*.

When we're tired, it's tough to stay present. Consequently, my marriage as well as many of my friendships suffered. My lack of inner stability was mirrored by many of my coworkers. It was as if they could serve in some of the world's most underserved and under-resourced cities and neighborhoods only as long as they knew they could go home for a short stay, take a quick holiday, or get out altogether. They were giving their all, but it wasn't a joyful, life-giving sort of sacrifice; it was more of an obligation or duty. Again, that exposed another inconsistency: we weren't able to follow through on all our commitments because we didn't have the inner strength to keep going.

We were perpetually teetering on the edge of burnout, and in fact quite a few of my coworkers did indeed burn out. Many gave up. Many left their serving communities. In the most tragic scenarios, some even walked away from their faith. Some of our belief systems simply weren't adequate to make sense of the suffering we witnessed. Our own doubts about the legitimacy of the notion of a good God in a world of hurt were too much for some of our supporters, pastoral caregivers, and even each other. And the havoc these doubts wreaked in our personal lives and relationships was often devastating.

It was a distant dream to think that people could actually love themselves, could actually be happy in demanding vocations, and could actually love to live in difficult places. It was a rare person among us who was able to make that crucial transition from allowing their vocation to be merely *sustainable* to developing it into something *thriving* and vibrant.

All of this caught up with me too. I had hurt myself and let down my community, and my wife suffered because of it. It was time to make a change. But it was an utter humiliation to realize that even my best efforts to be involved in meaningful, cause-driven social justice work had caused unintended harmful consequences. Eventually, I came to understand that many of those unforeseen consequences came from my subconscious and unconscious motivations.

One of the gifts of contemplation is that it facilitates a very gentle awakening to the misguided, selfish, and ego-driven impulses buried in our subconscious and unconscious. When we become awakened to these hidden motivations, we're able to mitigate some of those unintended harmful consequences; we're able to "do good better" (though of course we won't always get it right).

Through the support of teachers and guides, including Father Thomas and Father Richard, Phileena and I began to realize that grounding our social action in contemplative spirituality was the only way to ensure both personal and community wholeness. And that could only happen by nurturing solitude, silence, and stillness in our practice of prayer.

THE GIFTS OF SOLITUDE, SILENCE, AND STILLNESS

It's unfortunate that we tend to resist solitude, silence, and stillness, because some aspects of our awakening, growth, and development cannot be realized without them; each is a work of grace, a work only God can do in us.

We need practices that open us to this grace, this work of God.

God is love, and therefore God can be trusted. In silence, God will do for us what we cannot do for ourselves. So why are we afraid? Just be. Let go. Give in to the silence. Release the lies, the addictions, the temptations that keep you masked in your illusions.

This is easier said than done, but recognizing the inherent addictions that each of the Enneagram's three Intelligence Centers use to cope with their fears helps loosen the grasp of these interior compulsions. Gut people who are obsessed with *control*, heart people who are obsessed with *connections*, and head people who are obsessed with *competence* all need to find freedom from the ways they deal with their inner dread.

Aligning contemplative practices with this self-awareness brings about incredible personal liberation. Taking time to pause and create a spirituality marked by solitude, silence, and stillness reminds us who we truly are, in the best sense of our True Self.

While we need to cultivate all three, our Intelligence Center indicates one that is crucial for us.

For those in the Body Center, the gut people (types Eight, Nine, and One), *stillness* is crucial.

The Eight's driving energy, the Nine's dedication to mediation, and the One's desire to fix what is broken in the world are all important and unique gifts. But what happens when gut people simply stop? Who are they without the good they do? When an instinctive type is forced to stop, they realize how overidentified they are with their drive to *do*. They are not free.

STILLNESS

The gift of stillness refines the Body Center's instinctive drive to do by creating interior accountability for *proper* engagement in their active life. Stillness as a counterpoint to control brings forward freedom, and inner freedom loosens the grasp of gut people to impose their impassioned drive for good.

Stillness interrupts the addictions of gut people and prompts a reevaluation of their drive.

For those in the Heart Center, the feeling types, *solitude* is crucial.

Solitude functions as a correction to the feeling type's dependency on connection and comparison. Heart people who find themselves constantly drawn toward others for affirmation and approval are often still very lonely because they are disconnected from their essence. So then, who is the heart person when all alone? The Two who can't meet the needs of another? The Three who reads and reacts to the emotional energy of others to get what they want? The Four who longs to be seen and appreciated by others? When a heart type is disconnected from their essence they never feel fully embraced by others, leading to their experience of loneliness. The challenge is for those in the Heart Center to return to their essence and bring forward their True Self in relationship. Solitude is key to this recovery.

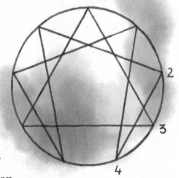

SOLITUDE

In solitude, a heart person's essence emerges in painfully liberating ways. Solitude teaches us how to be present—present to God, to ourselves, and to others with no strings attached. Presence in heart people allows for authentic connection to others, as well as to the past and the future, with a focus on the now.

For those in the Head Center, the thinking types, *silence* is crucial.

Is it possible for head people to turn down the inner noise—everything

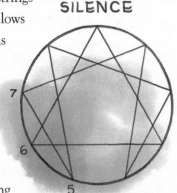

SILENCE

that serves as a distraction—to be able to really listen? Can the Five stop searching for answers long enough to hear the answer within? Can the Six stop worrying long enough to hear the quiet voice inside assuring them everything will be okay? Can the Seven dial down their anxious addiction to adventure and opportunity to hear that everything they need is already present?

Silence helps us learn how to listen to the voice of God in our lives, a voice we may have been unable to recognize before. Silence helps us listen to the people in our lives who speak loving words of truth or affirmation over us. And silence helps us to listen to ourselves—our desires and fears.

When we give ourselves to contemplative practices marked by solitude, silence, and stillness, our souls are nurtured, our Virtues blossom, and our True Self comes forward. Contemplative spirituality calms the body, stills the emotions, and quiets the mind. And in so doing, it liberates us from ego addictions, thereby giving us the freedom to make major corrections to our behaviors informed by our True Self.

The Enneagram shines a light on what obstructs our essence from emerging and opens our path to God. Contemplative spirituality then helps us overcome those obstacles hindering our awakening to the gift of our true identity.

CONTEMPLATION AND IDENTITY

One of the gifts of the contemplative life is acceptance. As we practice letting go, we learn to receive—all that is good within us as well as all that remains a challenge. Again, as Father Richard says, "Everything belongs." By pressing into our Basic Fears, we center ourselves more deeply and find that we don't have to react to those fears but can respond toward wholeness, toward growth, toward awakening.

We also learn to receive the gift of doubt as an invitation to press deeper into faith. Moving from belief to faith can cause anxiety. It drums up fear for some people, who feel they need to control their beliefs to be able to defend them or to rest confidently in them.

At its heart, faith is making the option for the absurd. What we're really doing is placing all our hope in the idea that these beliefs may in fact be true. The move from belief to faith is a move toward humility, a confessional move toward acceptance.

Ultimately, faith is learning to rest in mystery. But that invitation is a difficult one. So many of us spend much of our time trying to defend our beliefs, to come up with better arguments to convince someone that the way we think, live, act, or worship is superior. In those efforts we tend to gravitate toward arrogance.

Gentle as it is, the contemplative path is also severe, a demanding journey toward humility as we move from belief to faith. Contemplative spirituality holds us accountable by awakening us to the subconscious and unconscious motivations for what we are attempting to do in the context of our beliefs. It allows us to stay in the pain of our human condition yet not be overcome by it, keeping that pain from pushing us over the edge and instead allowing it to transform us.

Ultimately the goal of our journey with the Enneagram is to move from type to identity, to become rooted in dignity and reflect our essential True Self.

FRAGMENTS CLAIMING THE WHOLE

Who we think we are (in other words, our ideas about our identity) can be confused by the bits of our own narrative that we pick up and set down—the parts of our lives we're able to be truthful with ourselves about as well as those we continue to hide or refuse to face. These fragments of our unintegrated self compete for dominance, and often we allow one piece or another of our identity to lay claim to the whole of it.

We overidentify with the fragments we think are most attractive, the parts of our stories that seem most successful. This fragmentation keeps our shadow in the dark, out of sight and out of mind, yet always capable of sneaking up on us. For example, think of someone dominant in type Nine who overidentifies with the social role of a peacemaker. His community is harmonious because of his mediation efforts, yet his inner life is like a forgotten garden overgrown with weeds—ignored and disconnected from the whole. Or consider someone dominant in type Seven who overidentifies with her zeal. Her enthusiasm is so contagious that everyone loves to be around her, yet she can hardly stand being alone with herself, afraid she will suffocate from her personal pain. While she tries to take in as many positive experiences as life may offer, she doesn't let the good of those experiences penetrate deeply enough to heal her personal wounds.

A contemplative approach to the Enneagram invites us to resist the reductionism of inner fragmentation; to realize we aren't as bad as our worst moments or as good as our greatest successes—but that we are far better than we can imagine and carry the potential to be far worse than we fear. Father Richard once told me, "To cast great light in the world also requires a long shadow." Both belong. If we think we can run from the shadow, we're sorely mistaken; it is always with us. Facing the whole of ourselves rescinds the permission we give to the fragments to lay claim to the whole of our identity.

DIVINE AFFIRMATIONS AND
TRUTHFUL CONFRONTATION

Recall Henri Nouwen's three lies we discussed earlier in the book: "I am what I have," "I am what I do," "I am what other people say about me." Do you identify with one of these lies more than the others? Similarly, consider Thomas Keating's three programs for happiness: power and control, affection and esteem, and security and survival. Which resonates most strongly with you? These lies and programs can be understood as the fasteners that keep our masks stuck in place.

Now that we've come this far in learning to recognize our self beyond these lies and programs, how does our Enneagram path inform the way we nurture our spirituality? We can look to Jesus, who had to face these same lies and programs in his own way to reveal to us our original righteousness and True Self. Here is where these lies and illusions come full circle to meet their truth.

The similarities may be obvious when looking at Nouwen's three lies and Father Keating's three programs for happiness; they mirror each other and echo back to us our own human stories. What may be less obvious is the way these lies and programs for happiness show up as the subtext in the three temptations of Jesus.

In the fourth chapter of Matthew's Gospel we read the account of Jesus' fast when he was led by the Spirit of God into the desert or wilderness, where the liar (in Greek, *diabolos*, "the slanderer") hurled temptations at him for forty days and forty nights. The desert is clearly a symbol of retreat or withdrawal, an intentional moving into solitude, silence, and stillness to be tested—but what was actually being tested?

The three temptations of Jesus correlate directly to the three affirmations spoken over him following his baptism.

The first temptation, "If you are the Only Begotten, command these stones to turn into bread" (Matthew 4:3–4), gets at the lie *I am what I do* and the program for happiness of power and control. Certainly, if Jesus was God's Child, he should be able to demonstrate that through his spectacular power.

In the second temptation, the liar brings Jesus to the temple in Jerusalem and says, "If you are the Only Begotten, throw yourself down. Scripture has it, 'God will tell the angels to take care of you'" (Matthew 4:5–7). This is clearly a fortification of the lie *I am what others say about me* and the program for happiness of affection and esteem. Surely if Jesus was the Beloved, then God's affectionate care would never allow harm to befall him.

Finally, the liar shows Jesus the kingdoms of the world from a great mountaintop and promises, "All these I will give you if you fall down and worship me" (Matthew 4:8–10), a suggestion that supports the lie *I am what I have* and the program for happiness of security and survival. For if God truly was pleased, the reward would be the stability of security, a tangible sign that Jesus' preferred position would be established and recognized.

We still experience these lies today:

- If you're God's child, prove it! Do something. Show me your power and demonstrate who you are.
- If God loves you, test it! Jump and see if God will protect you. Show me how loved you really are.
- If God is pleased with you, show me the sign of favor! Show me the security symbol of God's pleasure.

The temptations not only align with the lies we learn to believe about our identities and the programs for happiness we become addicted to, but are direct confrontations of God's three affirmations of Jesus in the moments immediately *before* his forty days in the desert. At the end of the third chapter of Matthew's Gospel (3:13–17), Jesus is baptized, after which a voice from the heavens declares, "This is my Own [my child], my Beloved [whom I love], on whom my favor rests [with whom I am well pleased]" (v. 17).

Baptismal Affirmations		Temptation to Affirmation
This is my child	→	Turn stone to bread (prove your power)
Who is loved	→	Jump (if you're loved, you'll be rescued)
Upon whom favor rests	→	Bow down (your reward will symbolize your favor)

Ultimately, these affirmations become the antidote to the biggest lies about our identity. The self-awareness that the Enneagram generates, paired with contemplative practice, helps us hear these affirmations.

When we face the lie that we are what we have and in silence learn to listen, God says, "My pleasure over you is all you need."

When we stop our frenetic activity and face the lie that we are what we do, God says, "You are my beloved."

When we withdraw into our own interior solitude to face the lie that we are what others think, God says, "My child, rest in the grace of the truth that you belong to me."

These three Divine affirmations call forward the imprint of God within all humanity; they counter the classic and characteristic temptations supported by the delusional lies and addictive programs for happiness to which we've become enslaved. Because Christianity centers on the belief that Jesus was fully God and fully human, yet without sin, Jesus had to face these temptations to claim his identity as the Christ. And to loosen the grasp of the lies, he had to recover the loss of these affirmations in our shared human condition by illuminating the truth. How did Jesus do this? In self-deprivation he gave himself to the prayer practice of fasting in solitude, silence, and stillness, confronting any claims these lies or programs for happiness may have on the rest of us. In other words, Jesus does not ask us to do through contemplative practice what he has not done himself.

In the postures of solitude, silence, and stillness Jesus faced himself. The Divine affirmations spoken over him were tested through a slanderous interrogation that he overcame through truthful confrontation. Jesus allowed himself to stand in the face of antagonizing attacks against the truth of his own identity. His spirituality of *consent*, or agreeing to the intentions, required him to reclaim and recover presence by saying yes to his test. As Jesus intentionally *engaged* his belovedness, he willfully acknowledged something that is hard for many of us to accept about ourselves. Finally, when Jesus *rested*, giving himself the much-needed gift of finding his breath and savoring the present, he was able to recognize his own favored status.

PRAYING WITH OUR CENTERS

If identifying with the trials of Jesus is an invitation to union with God, then how do we allow this process to bring forth the inner integration we desperately need? How do we bring our whole self into our contemplative prayer practices? Where do we find the room to pray with the gifts of our Enneagram type's Intelligence Center?

Enneagram Intelligence Centers	Nouwen's Lies	Keating's Programs	Jesus' Temptations	Contemplative Prayer Posture
Gut/Body Type Eight Type Nine Type One	"I am what I do."	Power + Control	"Tell these stones to become bread."	Stillness (Engagement)
Heart/Emotions Type Two Type Three Type Four	"I am what others say or think about me."	Affection + Esteem	"Throw yourself down."	Solitude (Presence)
Head/Mind Type Five Type Six Type Seven	"I am what I have."	Security + Survival	"All this I will give you."	Silence (Listening)

1. **Unmask the lies of our identity**, as taught by Father Henri Nouwen: "I am what I have," "I am what I do," and "I am what other people say or think about me." Nouwen's three lies line up perfectly with each of the Enneagram's three Intelligence Centers. Identifying the lie to which our center is most susceptible is the first step in learning to pray with what tempts us at the core.

2. **Loosen the grasp of our addictions to programs for happiness**, as taught through Father Thomas Keating's three basic psychological needs to be met for our personal development: power and control; affection and esteem; and security and survival. These three programs for happiness line up perfectly with the Basic Fears of each of the Enneagram's three Intelligence Centers. Examining the program for happiness to which our center is most susceptible opens us up to learning how to let go of our addictive compulsions that support our Basic Fears.

3. **Recognize our temptations.** We've seen how the three temptations of Christ during his forty days of fasting in the desert line up perfectly with the prime identity lies of each of the Enneagram's three Intelligence Centers. In examining the temptation toward the Fixation of our center, we find gentle invitations into the essential qualities and original innocence of our Enneagram types.

4. **Map contemplative prayer postures with our Intelligence Centers.** Charting out Nouwen's lies, Keating's programs for happiness, and the temptations of Christ with the Enneagram's three Intelligence Centers clearly shows patterns for spiritual growth. By aligning contemplative prayer postures (solitude, silence, and stillness) with our Intelligence Centers (which by now we see are also aligned with our lies of identity, programs for happiness, and temptations), we obtain a roadmap for spiritual postures and practices that support our unique path to spiritual growth.

Mapping Your Enneagram Type *with* Your Unique Path *to* Spiritual Growth

Integrating Knowledge with Practice

If you've made it this far, you're ready to find your unique path to spiritual growth. The pilgrimage home to God involves three phases: a *construction* phase of identity, followed by an earth-shattering *deconstruction* of who we thought we were, which finally brings us to the necessary *reconstruction* of something truer.

In this journey we started with construction: learning about the Enneagram, discovering the way it is centered in triads, exploring the character-structure components, and reviewing the particularities of the nine types. A lot of people stop here, content in the construction phase, happy to understand the constructs of their identity. In this phase we find the contours of the shape of our sense of self. This self-awareness is crucial if we are to progress to the next phase.

During the deconstruction phase of the book, we learned that some of the aspects of our sense of self are tethered to Nouwen's lies, Keating's programs for happiness, and the temptations of Jesus. And if we dare to wake up from the illusory aspects of our self-realized container, we can wade through the muddy mess of deconstruction, realizing our identity is not ultimately found in what we do, what we have, or what others say about us.

Now it's time to step into reconstruction, where we'll find signposts to help us navigate the reordering of our identity into wholeness. As we shall see, these signposts are rooted in contemplative spirituality and practice, without which we will stumble around between deconstruction and construction, fumbling to grasp a grounded sense of self and reality. But with contemplative practice as our companion and guide, we will find faith and courage to become who we were before the assault on our original righteousness or Virtue occurred.

INTEGRATING SOLITUDE, SILENCE, AND STILLNESS WITH OUR CENTERS

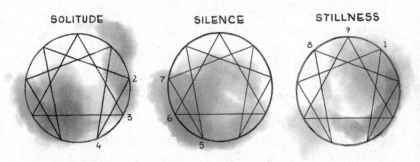

Contemplative practice confronts our resistance to being present, in the now. Usually we lack presence because we are preoccupied with something in our future that we actually need to be practicing presence for today. Other times we lack presence because we are fixated on our past, regretting what is now out of our control. But rooting our self in presence is what leads to the balance and integrity of integrating our Head, Heart, and Body Centers.

At first, solitude, silence, and stillness trigger the most accessible emotion of each of the centers (anxiety or distress for the head types, guilt or shame for the heart types, and anger or frustration for the body types). This is the beginning of unlocking the door to your path of spiritual growth, so don't be dissuaded by the resistance you initially experience.

Contemplative prayer is difficult; it requires practice. When Jesus reminds us to be like children, it is a clue that all of us will be lifelong beginners on the spiritual journey. Moving from practice to discipline is where we start to see the fruit of freedom from the lies, programs, and temptations. But listen to yourself: usually the way you judge yourself or "feel bad" about your practice is the very thing that begins to open your type to the graces of the practice.

Fundamentally what we are doing here is *excavating our essence*, our True Self, from the lies, programs, and temptations we've wrapped around our identity. We do this by practicing presence, by showing up with our whole self to the God who lovingly seeks to shape and restore us. Being truly present requires establishing a particular prayer posture in contemplative practice.

Remember, contemplative prayer is marked by the postures of solitude, silence, and stillness. As it turns out, the Intelligence Centers—our way of *seeing* the world—uniquely align themselves to each posture: the Heart Center types require solitude, the Head Center types must use silence, and the Body Center types need to engage in stillness.

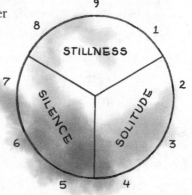

These postures aren't just how we bring ourselves to prayer—they are the entryway to a mindful life, to an awakened *attention* to God's love which is always near, always present.

INTEGRATING CONSENT, ENGAGEMENT, AND REST WITH OUR HARMONY TRIAD

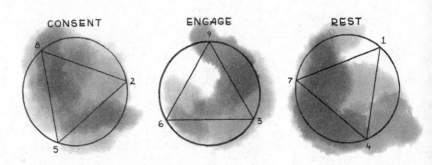

Just as our Intelligence Center uniquely aligns with one of the prayer postures, our Harmony Triad—as our way of *engaging* the world—uniquely aligns with a particular prayer *intention* (consent, engagement, or rest).

The *posture* is a practice in itself, but our *intention* reverberates with our "heart"—the organ of spiritual perception. Our intention points to what our heart needs most in order to connect with God. Our intention—whether consent, engagement, or rest—is the particular way we (like my puppy Basil) metaphorically roll over onto our back and open the most vulnerable part of our self to the God who is safe and loves us unconditionally.

Simply put, when speaking of the intentions for our spiritual practice we are identifying the inner disposition we bring to our contemplative prayer posture.

Giving *attention* to our posture allows an *intention* to emerge. Maybe it's *consenting* to God's love for you—no longer trying to earn it (Two), figure it out (Five), or resist it (Eight), but just letting it wash over you. Or maybe it's *engaging* God's love—making it the source of your affirmation (Three), allowing it to silence your fears (Six), or letting it bring an inner, grounding peace (Nine). Finally, it may simply be *resting* in God's love—receiving it as the ultimate source of goodness (One), seeing your belovedness in it (Four), or allowing rest to become freedom, the gift it was always meant to be (Seven).

	Harmony Triad	Dominant Affect Group	Prayer Posture	Prayer Intention
Type One	Idealist	Frustration Type	Stillness	Rest
Type Two	Relationist	Rejection Type	Solitude	Consent
Type Three	Pragmatist	Attachment Type	Solitude	Engage
Type Four	Idealist	Frustration Type	Solitude	Rest
Type Five	Relationist	Rejection Type	Silence	Consent
Type Six	Pragmatist	Attachment Type	Silence	Engage
Type Seven	Idealist	Frustration Type	Silence	Rest
Type Eight	Relationist	Rejection Type	Stillness	Consent
Type Nine	Pragmatist	Attachment Type	Stillness	Engage

But unlike the intuitive draw toward what may seem an obvious prayer posture for our Intelligence Center, our prayer intentions are harder to identify. In a sense, our prayer intention is hidden from us, keeping us stuck in the loops that tether us to our illusions. This is one more way the Harmony Triads expose to us the "hidden wholeness" of the Enneagram—they show us what we need most in prayer.*

---

* Angela Griner, EdD, of the Department of Education at Rollins College in Orlando, Florida, and Stacey Griner, MPH, CPH, of the Department of Community and Family Health at the University of South Florida, aided in conducting an Enneagram and prayer research project documented in *Enneagram and Spiritual Practice* (http://gravitycenter.com/enneagramandspiritualpractice/). Of the 538 survey respondents, most reported they were very familiar (38.8 percent) or somewhat familiar (50.4 percent) with their type and the Enneagram types in general. Similarly, most were very familiar (44.6 percent) or somewhat familiar (44.8 percent) with contemplative spirituality. The survey demonstrated that given the options of solitude, silence, and stillness for preferred prayer postures, the majority of respondents in the Head Center chose silence, the majority of respondents in the Heart Center chose solitude, and the majority of those in the Body Center chose stillness. However,

One of the great difficulties of the contemplative journey is acknowledging that we need our intention to be supported by our prayer posture. Such an acknowledgment assumes a tremendous level of self-awareness regarding what is required for us to find freedom and flourish. What's so remarkable is that the Enneagram helps awaken this self-awareness and reveals what our particular type needs to come alive and thrive.

ALIGNING CONTEMPLATIVE INTENTIONS WITH THE HARMONY TRIADS

What do you need most from God? How does holding your contemplative prayer posture with a prayer intention help you find your way home using the sacred map of the Enneagram? Essentially, how each Harmony Triad relates to the world is the key to understanding how each might best relate to their spiritual formation.

Consent, engagement, and rest are the intentions that help us find our way home. When these intentions are combined with the postures of solitude, silence, and stillness, we start to wake up from our illusions. Matching intentions with the Harmony Triads (how we relate to the world) and postures with the Intelligence Centers (how we perceive the world) creates nine unique intention + posture combinations that correlate with what each type needs to discover freedom and find wholeness.

For types Two, Five, and Eight, the Relationists, the intention is *consent*. For types Three, Six, and Nine, the Pragmatists, the intention is *engagement*. For types One, Four, and Seven, the Idealists, the intention is *rest*.

---

given consent, engage, and rest as options for preferred intentions, respondents didn't show a clear pattern. The study confirmed that people can more easily discern what their prayer posture should be based on their Intelligence Center; however, the study also confirmed that the prayer intentions for the Harmony Triads are harder to discern. This points to the need to help people discover the appropriate prayer intention in their spiritual formation.

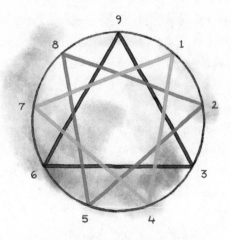

REST CONSENT ENGAGE

Consent as the Prayer Intention for the Harmony Triads' Relationists

Because the Relationists (the Dominant Affect Groups' Rejection types) avoid acknowledging their needs by denying or rejecting them, their invitation to prayer involves consenting to the gift of having needs. When the Relationists own what they want, they allow themselves to receive without reservation.

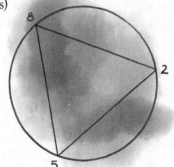

Consent is more than acquiescence. Consent is active agreement, the agreement to give of yourself, though not at your expense or in a way that diminishes you, but rather as an offering of love. Consent is saying yes to more of everything that helps facilitate your coming home, your liberation.

Twos, Fives, and Eights reject their needs in their poor attempt to get what they don't have. So these rejection types need to learn to consent to what they *do* have by agreeing it is enough.

When Twos consent to solitude, they agree to be alone in order to stop trying to please everyone—even God. Twos who constantly attempt to delight God fill all the surrounding space with their insecure energy and so are unable to receive Divine Love, which is already reaching toward them, even within them. Twos who withdraw to solitude consent to be present to God rather than to please God, which allows them to be filled by God with the love they long for.

When Fives consent to silence, they are choosing to trust that God will still be there when their mind is at rest. If it's true that God's first language is silence, then when Fives quiet their minds, they have an opportunity to listen to the voice of God. By consenting to silence, Fives find freedom through mystery—an irony to the Five whose illusion perpetuates the lie that freedom will be found in answers.

Because no one can convince them to stop, when Eights consent to stillness, they *choose* to agree to stop. They opt to let go of their need to be in control and instead trust in God.

When Twos, Fives, and Eights consent to what they perpetually reject, they are able to receive the gifts of solitude, silence, and stillness, and at last find healing for the fragmented self.

Engagement as the Prayer Intention for the Harmony Triads' Pragmatists

Because the Pragmatists (the Dominant Affect Groups' Attachment types) hold on to what it is they desire (admiration, confidence, harmony) as a way of fortifying the illusions of their ego constructs, engagement is the prayer intention that loosens their grasp.

Engagement means showing up, intentionally being aware of

our needs by resisting the tendency toward resignation. Engagement is especially important for the Pragmatists, because as Anchor Points, they are the most disconnected from their Intelligence Center. For the Pragmatists, who also happen to be the Anchor Points, engaging or reengaging with their center is the first step in their journey to wholeness and integration.

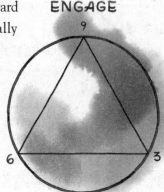

Threes, Sixes, and Nines attach to what they believe works (but really just keeps them disconnected), so their invitation is to learn to engage what they already have.

When Threes engage solitude, they access a part of their heart that seems to have been lost. Threes need to engage solitude as a gift, not detaching from relationships to fuel the addiction of self-nurturing. Threes who are able to face themselves alone, being in the present moment, dismantle their Fixation of vanity.

When Sixes engage silence as a way of overcoming fear, their inner courage emerges. Many Sixes find silence painful because it amplifies the powerful lies fear tells them. Sixes may be afraid of being present to inner silence, but interrogating silence allows them to hear what they otherwise can't hear within themselves.

When Nines engage stillness, they discover their profound attention to their intention. Nines need to step into stillness as a conscious intention to show up and be present to God.

Engaging solitude, silence, and stillness is the antidote to the addictive patterns of retreat that Threes, Sixes, and Nines use to detach from their center. For these Anchor Points, the gifts of mindful awareness emerge as conscious participation in prayer develops.

Rest as the Prayer Intention for the Harmony Triads' Idealists

Finally, the Idealists (the Dominant Affect Groups' Frustration types) will never attain their unrealistic idealized notions of what they desire. Always teetering between resignation and resistance, they find themselves perpetually exhausted both inside and out. Though they deserve it as much as anyone, the Idealists never allow themselves the much-needed respite required to find the truth of who they really are.

Rest meets the deepest needs of the Idealists, who are continually agitated, never satisfied, and often upset with themselves for failing to live into their impossible standards of excellence (One), originality (Four), or flexibility (Seven). Rest gives Ones, Fours, and Sevens a break from their constant frustration.

When Ones rest in stillness, they find their breath and let themselves off the hook for not always getting everything perfect. It's okay for Ones to stop fixing everything, themselves included, and relax.

It's important for Fours to rest in solitude, to know being alone is okay. When Fours dial down the intensity of their emotional energy, they finally understand that their own inner angst can be too much even for them to bear. Allowing themselves to rest from all the inner turmoil enables them to come back to their relationships with clarity and inner calm.

When Sevens rest in silence, they find the greatest adventures already lie within their own souls. Sevens don't need to run off to what's next when they learn to listen to what's within. Caricatured as the type that is always up, always on the move, and always dreaming,

Sevens are prone to the eventuality of burnout, so turning off all the noise of options and opportunity is critical. Silence minimizes the distractions of all the great ideas Sevens find themselves drowning in.

Resting in solitude, silence, and stillness restores these frustrated souls' lost idealism. It remedies the immature naïveté in Ones, Fours, and Sevens who are the Enneagram's most fatigued fanatics and frayed advocates for a better world full of integrity (One), beauty (Four), and freedom (Seven).

INTRODUCING HOW THE HEART TYPES
ALIGN SOLITUDE WITH INTENTION

For the heart types, opting to slip away, to nurture spaces for not just interior solitude but actual aloneness, and to create opportunities to practice presence in seclusion may seem painfully isolating, but it is fertile ground for awakening. Practices carried out in solitude combat the fears of not being loved, seen, or understood; confront the lie "I am what others say or think about me"; and loosen the addictive grasp that affection and esteem have in and through this center.

Solitude allows heart types to savor the present by quieting the flurry of their emotions, thereby bringing balance. For many heart types, solitude is a trigger to deeper experiences of loneliness, but in solitude the fears associated with being alone can be faced without distractions. In this way, solitude heals even the most tender cracks in the hearts of the Feeling Center types.

In *consenting to solitude*, those dominant in type Two find freedom from the inner drive to meet the needs of those they love, allowing their own needs to be seen (by themselves and God) and met. For type Three, *engaging solitude* is a form of promise-keeping, facing their inner truth and living into it. For type Four, *resting in solitude* is a retreat from their constant attractional energy, offering them a reprieve from their inner critic so they can savor themselves in the present.

INTRODUCING HOW THE HEAD TYPES
ALIGN SILENCE WITH INTENTION

Those in the Head Center, the types most dialed into figuring out and preventing threats to certainty, safety, and freedom, require a healthy dose of silence to quiet the constant churning of their thoughts. In the peace of inner quiet, head types can hear the truth that they have enough, refuting the lie "I am what I have" and loosening the addictive grasp that security and survival have in and through this center.

SILENCE

7

6

5

Silence brings clarity to the overactive mind always convoluted by its hunt for answers (Five), assurance (Six), or access (Seven). When we turn down the inner distractions and learn to listen to our breath, our body, our instincts, and the voice of God, we are able to hear what we've always known: that we are enough, that we have enough, and that God is enough. There can be no greater security than resting in the truth of what is told to us in silence.

For type Five, *consenting to silence* is the grace of letting go of the compulsions of their drive, which is always demanding solutions and answers, thereby allowing mystery to be their guide. For type Six, *engaging silence* is a way of confronting their fear of being quiet. For type Seven, *resting in silence* helps muffle the ever-persistent, future-forward mental activity that frustrates their ability to remain content in the present moment.

INTRODUCING HOW THE GUT TYPES ALIGN STILLNESS WITH INTENTION

For the gut or body types, slowing down, creating intentional pauses, and in some cases simply ceasing all activity become the correction to what is out of control in their active lives. Practices marked by stillness help dismantle the lie "I am what I do" and loosen the addictive grasp that power and control have in and through this center.

Stillness teaches us restraint, preparing us for proper engagement and compassionate action. For active Body Center types, achieving an inner state of stillness requires a practice of grounded presence and receptivity. This isn't to suggest that Body Center types always need to withdraw or even find a quiet place to practice stillness. For many of these individuals, stillness starts with slowing down, finding their breath, and feeling their bodies, taking deliberate steps while walking or mindful bites while eating. Inner stillness helps body types to observe their compulsions and loosens the grasp these ego addictions have on their behaviors.

For those dominant in type Eight, *consenting to stillness* is simply the practice of saying yes, a gentle agreement to stop and be present.

For type Nine, *engaging stillness* is a reminder to be intentional about their inner calm, not merely to opt out or check out but to be attentive to the gift of stillness as a discipline. For type One, *resting in stillness* is the tender gift of permission—permission to take a break from all of their inner frustration and resentment.

FROM COMPLEXITY TO PRACTICAL SIMPLICITY

We've come now to the apex of our exploration of the Enneagram for spiritual formation, its sacred nature. We've seen how our Intelligence Center informs our particular prayer posture and how our Harmony Triad informs our particular intention. When we overlay these two triads, nine unique combinations of contemplative prayer postures + prayer intentions emerge.

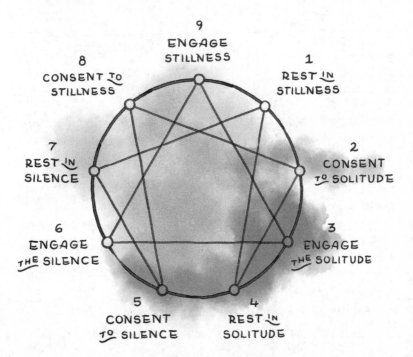

These type-specific postures and intentions provide ground-breaking application for working with the Enneagram for spiritual growth. Moving from complexity to practical simplicity, here are the nine ways to return to our True Self:

Type One	Rest in Stillness
Type Two	Consent to Solitude
Type Three	Engage Solitude
Type Four	Rest in Solitude
Type Five	Consent to Silence
Type Six	Engage Silence
Type Seven	Rest in Silence
Type Eight	Consent to Stillness
Type Nine	Engage Stillness

As you can see, the path home for your type is simple. It just requires your participation. In the next chapter we'll explore these paths home in more detail.

9

The Way Home

Mapping the Nine Types with New Ways to Pray

Self-awareness is the beginning of liberation, but becoming stalled in a self-gazing posture quickly leads to a form of narcissism. Once we move beyond type as a mere caricature of personality traits, we are ready to work with the Enneagram for spiritual growth. Getting to the reasons *why* we stay stuck in the patterns that keep us tethered to our illusions offers clarity for specifically *how* to pray with our type for true freedom. So, what do these nine paths back to our True Self look like, and what do they entail?

THE WAY HOME FOR TYPE ONE:
Rest in Stillness

Intelligence Center	Body/Gut/Instinctive
Harmony Triad	Idealist
Dominant Affect Group	Frustration
Prayer Posture	Stillness
Prayer Intention	Rest

Learning to develop compassion for oneself is crucial for Ones who live in their bodies as a prison of unattainable perfection, a place of perpetual disappointment as a result of their unrealistic expectations.

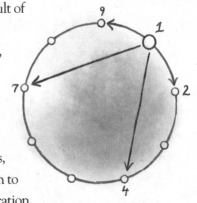

To press into greater freedom, Ones need to welcome the tension and frustration they carry in their bodies—often played out through the grinding of their jaws while sleeping, the knots in their backs, and the stress headaches they learn to live with—as invitations to integration.

Like the other gut types, Ones will always be tempted to think they are "what they do," specifically as it relates to fixing all the brokenness in the world, correcting everything they deem wrong, and aligning the world with the goodness they desire to see flourish.

As Idealists, Ones believe they can fix all that is flawed, and this notion drives them to the end of themselves with an insatiable idealism they can't let go of without feeling they're losing part of their own essence. This is why *stillness* is crucial for Ones—although the simple invitation to stop, even for a moment, can seem impossible. But if Ones don't stop, they'll drive themselves off the ledge into a deep place of anger with themselves for not living up to their own standards—an anger that is subsequently peddled outward toward others (though the rest of us get only the leftovers after they've beaten themselves up).

Because the intensity of this drive compels Ones to keep moving, the prayer intention of *rest* allows them to return to the gifts of the present moment in all the ways they nurture their spirituality. Rest is urgent to dial down their movement, balance their energy, and slow down their drive so that stillness can be a place of renewal. As part of the Dominant Affect Groups' Frustration types, when Ones fail to externalize the impossibility of their internalized standards, not only do they project their irritation into their environments, but they end up having to pick up the pieces of the damaged relationships resulting from such misdirected frustrations.

The fundamental move for people dominant in type One is from frustration to rest, from their addictive compulsions for perfection to the peace of their traditional Virtue, *serenity*.

Ultimately, people dominant in type One need to learn to *rest in stillness*. Stillness for Ones connects them to the reality of who they are by calming the emotional energy of their anger and releasing the mental vise grip in which their resentment holds them. In stillness, they learn to rest, to stop trying to fix everything and correct everyone, and to arrest their own inner criticisms and judgment. Ones have to receive stillness as a gift, a much-needed breather, allowing it to nurture inner tranquility through a conscious cessation from their perfectionistic drive.

THE WAY HOME FOR TYPE TWO:
Consent to Solitude

Intelligence Center	Heart/Feeling/Emotion
Harmony Triad	Relationist
Dominant Affect Group	Rejection
Prayer Posture	Solitude
Prayer Intention	Consent

Of all types, the Two operates from the heart more than any other. Those dominant in type Two are the feelings-forward people who bathe the world in love and genuine kindness.

But it is difficult for Twos to return to their own hearts because they spend so much of their energy tending to the hearts of others— especially those types who are disconnected and distant from their

Feeling Center. Because Twos naturally succumb to the lie that they
are "what others think or say
about them," they will fuel this
temptation with subconscious
compulsions to form ever deeper
and more intimate connections
to prove that they are truly loving.

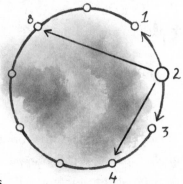

Because Twos are Relationists,
not only will this initiative to intertwine themselves in people's lives
keep them externally focused, but it will distract them from being
truthful with themselves about their own needs and the shame they
feel when forced to face or acknowledge those needs.

Since Twos are so given to relational connections and compar-
isons with others, *solitude* will at first be painful for them. Who is
the Two apart from their relationships? Solitude may cause Twos to
finally connect with the pain in their own heart of feeling isolated
or uncared for in the ways they long to be shown love. But after time,
solitude will become their greatest companion, allowing them to
listen to the voice within that has always been there, reminding them
they have all the love they need because they are a source of love.

For those Twos who are naturally introverted, solitude might seem
a welcome stance. But since Twos are driven by saying yes to the needs
of others, it's not easy for them to say yes to themselves. This is why
consent is the critical intention for the Two. Initially, consent—agreeing
to say yes to being alone in solitude—will be met with tremendous
resistance. But Twos must consent to solitude in order to unmask the
lie "I am what others think or say about me." Consenting, or giving
themselves, to solitude confronts their addiction to giving themselves
away externally while seldom facing what awaits them within.

As a Rejection type in the Dominant Affect Groups, Twos find that consenting to their own needs increases their willingness to be honest about these needs, because in the end, rejecting the possibility that anyone else could help meet their needs will only drive them deeper away from their essence.

Fundamentally, in consenting to solitude, Twos learn to rest in the grace that they are loved for who they are, not for what they offer the rest of us.

Ultimately, the Twos' invitation is to *consent to solitude* by making an agreement with themselves that it's okay to be alone. The choice to consent isn't a passive showing up or a defeated withdrawal; it's an intentional choice to be present to themselves and their needs. Taking the focus off others can feel awkward for Twos, because they find their identities wrapped up in how they are mirrored by others. So solitude invites them into new ways of introspection and presence, causing them to face their own fears of abandonment and their resistance to intentional isolation. Prayers of consent to solitude help Twos surrender their need to give, serve, and love outwardly to find themselves. Practicing solitude awakens their essence as the beloved.

THE WAY HOME FOR TYPE THREE:
Engage Solitude

Intelligence Center	Heart/Feeling/Emotion
Harmony Triad	Pragmatist
Dominant Affect Group	Attachment
Prayer Posture	Solitude
Prayer Intention	Engage

As the Anchor Point of the feeling types, Threes experience a separation from their hearts and distance from their emotions. (Recall that Threes, Sixes, and Nines are the types most disconnected from their Intelligence Center.) Because of this emotional disconnect, Threes almost seem to observe their feelings at arm's length. However, Threes still have a highly developed intuition for reading the emotional energy of those around them, which allows them to relate to all kinds of people on a myriad of levels.

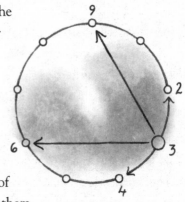

Coming home for the Three requires facing their feelings, listening to the subtext of their emotional intelligence, and engaging their own hearts without judgment or prejudice. In so doing they can overcome the lie of their identity, "I am what others think or say about me," and their Childhood Wound—their malformed perception of love, which seems tucked underneath the admiration of others.

In relating to the world as Pragmatists (the Harmony Triads' Threes, Sixes, and Nines), Threes may be tethered to the addiction of casting aside their feelings as not practical enough or not sensible enough to aid in making clearheaded decisions. This is where they stay stuck. Appealing to their other centers will lead to integration, but only after they've integrated the gift of their own heart.

Solitude then is the contemplative invitation for Threes to find themselves. In solitude Threes don't have to look for admiration to find the shape of their identity. In solitude they learn they don't need to prove to God their value, or perform for God to be validated, or need to be seen as worthy before God to pray. Just being alone, trusting that God is near, is their grace.

For many Threes, solitude may seem easy since emotional reservation or detachment is part of the hustle, part of the strategy of observing their environment to determine how they are perceived and therefore how they need to adjust to be loved. *Engaging solitude* is where Threes will find difficulty, but ultimately their liberation, because engaging solitude forces them to discover who they are apart from the perceptions of others. But really engaging, really showing up in solitude, being awake in it and aware of it, is what will shake loose all the illusions about themselves they try to convince the rest of us to believe are true.

Threes are an Attachment type in the Dominant Affect Groups with a proclivity to perform for others' attention, so detaching from external sources through solitude forces them to listen to the voice of Love within that provides all the nurturing validation they need.

When Threes are centered, their truthfulness radiates an unyielding hope that makes way for the possibility of a rooted and authentic sense of self, not dependent on hollow validations, but affirmed by God's love.

As fluent as Threes appear to be socially, many note that they find themselves revitalized by disengaging and removing themselves from the public. The distance Threes need from relationships and communities can be a way of coping with their own inner pain of feeling disconnected from their hearts. Thus, for many Threes the idea of solitude is a welcome change to their highly visible lives. But the invitation to *engage solitude* requires Threes to be really present in their solitude rather than checking out or getting lost in it. Engaging solitude allows them the rare opportunity to look inward at the truth of their value. It offers Threes an opportunity to discover their own significance apart from the admiration they chase to help them feel valuable.

THE WAY HOME FOR TYPE FOUR:
Rest in Solitude

Intelligence Center	Heart/Feeling/Emotion
Harmony Triad	Idealist
Dominant Affect Group	Frustration
Prayer Posture	Solitude
Prayer Intention	Rest

Fours almost seem to drown in their hearts as a way of relating to the intensity of their emotions. In their feelings they experience a magnetic draw toward deep sorrow and deep joy—feelings that remind them they are alive, while everything around them seems to be dying.

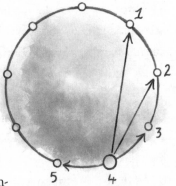

When Fours come home to themselves, they welcome the courage to explore the fullness of their hearts. Fours have huge hearts, encompassing all the emotions that could possibly be contained within a heart. Yet the heart of the Four is a paradox; it can seem remarkably present to itself while simultaneously seeming to be cut off from itself. The near-yet-distant heart of the Four fuels the lie "I am what other people think or say about me."

Fours desire to be seen for who they want to be or who they hope they are. They are searching for their identity and want others to see it and affirm it in themselves. Thus, being seen is of critical importance. And sometimes they get stuck there.

Fours have a natural tendency to feel too much, causing them to think they *are* their feelings. Fours know every contour of their feelings. In fact, Fours probably came up with the "feeling words" list. They are the most proficient at identifying the color of feelings, and since their emotions can be so overwhelming, they tend to fall asleep in the illusion that what they feel is more real than reality itself. And so, the self-centered fantasy that Fours create is what shackles them to their False Self.

As Idealists, Fours never quite attain what they desire, which becomes a self-perpetuating source of sadness. It may come as bad news to the Four, but what they desperately need is to bring the posture of *solitude* to their contemplative prayer practices, disciplining themselves to be alone and unseen so that they can wake up and learn to see themselves for who they truly are.

Certainly, solitude might pander to introverted Fours, so they must be careful not to allow it to become another escape or coping technique but instead a place of *rest* from the compulsion to be seen. This allows Fours to take a break from their unrealistic idealism and the constant frustration rooted in their Dominant Affect Group style that reminds them no one nor any experience will ever fulfill their idealized hopes.

Ultimately, Fours must move from desiring to be known (by themselves and others) to resting in the gift of their composed, self-actualized, unshakable True Self.

Many Fours find themselves feeling isolated, and so the notion of solitude is a familiar one, but being able to *rest in solitude* is the distinction Fours need to apply. For people dominant in type Four, resting in solitude is a means of retreat, a departure from the strains and demands in their lives. In seclusion, Fours find freedom to explore the depth of their vast emotional capacity as a way to investigate their inner world. But Fours bring their frustration inward, so when a Four can relax that frustration and *rest*, then solitude becomes a place of healing and wholeness. Turning down their anguish, retreating from their sorrow, and breathing into their yearning to be known offers the soothing restoration found only in communion with God.

THE WAY HOME FOR TYPE FIVE:
Consent to Silence

Intelligence Center	Head/Mind/Thinking
Harmony Triad	Relationist
Dominant Affect Group	Rejection
Prayer Posture	Silence
Prayer Intention	Consent

Frequently mistaken as lost in their heads, Fives are the most rooted in their mental realm. They may appear like an absentminded professor, but don't be mistaken; there's nothing absentminded about them; Fives take in everything through their mental faculties. They are always alert, keenly aware of all they can absorb and reflect on to make sense of reality in their pursuit of security.

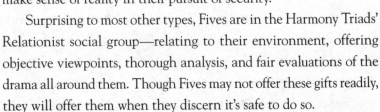

Surprising to most other types, Fives are in the Harmony Triads' Relationist social group—relating to their environment, offering objective viewpoints, thorough analysis, and fair evaluations of the drama all around them. Though Fives may not offer these gifts readily, they will offer them when they discern it's safe to do so.

Though Fives can recognize a lie with precise lucidity, they still tend to believe the lie that "they are what they have," a belief that propels their compulsion toward mental activity and problem solving. Indeed, "I am what I have; I have the answers" is the defining illusion for the Five.

Coming home for Fives requires a detachment from their mental preoccupations. Contemplative practice can seem easy, given their proclivity toward introversion. But though they may welcome the challenge to figure out the fruit of practice, they might do so without actually having practiced the prayer. Therefore, *silence* is necessary for Fives to turn down the exhausting, mental obsession with finding answers.

When the Five can *consent* to silence—essentially giving themselves permission to detach from mental activity—they are at last able to connect with God. But having overidentified with the buzz of activity in their minds, silence can be difficult and painful. *Who am I if I don't have the answers?*

As a Rejection type in the Dominant Affect Groups, Fives find that consenting to silence heals the external denunciation they constantly experience. They often feel rejected by others while at the same time are obsessed with rejecting what they perceive to be the intrusions of others into their head space. The quiet control that Fives exert over their inner lives allows them to resist external intrusions, but this rejection of social imposition keeps them stuck in their heads. Though Fives appear to be among the most reserved of all Enneagram types, the constant churning of questions in their minds creates persistent noise that only silence can remedy.

For people dominant in type Five, silence is the posture that allows them to learn to consent as an intention. To *consent to silence* for Fives means to be present to the silence as an agreement, to intentionally make room for it amid their compulsive mental interrogations. Rather than merely checking out, when Fives make room for silence in true consent they permit Divine interruptions and sacred answers to supersede their own ability to offer what they deem the most sensible solutions to life's greatest questions. Consenting to silence helps Fives realize they are accepted as they are and safe in the unknown, even if they don't have all the answers.

In the end, when Fives can consent to silence, they wake up to Mystery, no longer distracted by the mental noise they've created as a way to avoid their fear of not finding solutions. By saying yes to silence, they find a way of living more freely, not emotionally or mentally detached, but unattached to needing to be the bearer of answers to make the world safe.

THE WAY HOME FOR TYPE SIX:
Engage Silence

Intelligence Center	Head/Mind/Thinking
Harmony Triad	Pragmatist
Dominant Affect Group	Attachment
Prayer Posture	Silence
Prayer Intention	Engage

Though they are in the middle of the Head Center, Sixes are the most disconnected from their rational mind. Being unrooted in reason, they give way to anxiety-ridden, irrational conundrums, perpetuating the lack of peace they commonly experience. Fear is the life preserver that Sixes think will keep them from drowning, and all the

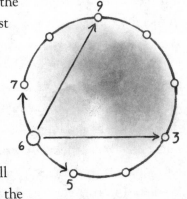

mental anxiety produced is the dysfunctional pool that keeps them afloat. Paradoxically, when Sixes turn to their rational faculties to avoid facing their fears, their fear usually only escalates. Mental anxiety is their addiction.

Like the other head types, Sixes fall prey to the lie "I am what I have." The Six is compelled to have security. The quintessential threat forecaster, the Six compulsively creates contingency plans for everything and everyone they care about. This brings them to imagine the worst possible scenarios, leaving them in a panicky, frenzied state of mind.

For Sixes to come home, they must learn to face their fears by reconnecting with their Intelligence Center: the mind. By grounding themselves in the mind, Sixes can face their fears rationally and realize that everything they fear is rooted in the illusion that keeps them asleep.

Sixes are among the Harmony Triads' Pragmatists; thus, if something makes sense to Sixes, then their inherent need for trust causes them to attach to it. But as soon as whatever it is that once made sense to them becomes a source of confusion, Sixes will abandon logic and move away from or against the confusion, which is viewed as a threat.

Constant threat forecasting keeps Sixes distracted, unable to connect with the gift of the present moment and incapable of hearing the voice of God. But when Sixes emphasize *silence* as their contemplative prayer posture, they are forced to turn down the noise of all their inner anxiety and listen to what is true, what has always been true within them—that they are going to be okay because ultimately they are a source of courage.

Engaging silence is their path forward on the spiritual journey. As a prayer intention, engagement in the face of silence draws forward the Six's courage. It challenges the Six not to back down or comply with their apprehensions, waking them up to their own courage.

To keep distance from their anxiety, typical Sixes avoid silence. Already mistrusting of themselves, they don't want to fall deeper into their fears where the silence is deafening and only amplifies their inner distress. But when Sixes *engage silence*, something happens— they hear the truth about who they are: strong and resilient heroes and sheroes. Occupying silence with their courage allows for Sixes to participate in the ways that silence cleanses them of doubt, eases their worries, and quiets their suspicions. Silence heals the fractured strength of Sixes when they muster up the audacity to engage it with their whole self. Engaging silence validates the daring valor that the panicky cognizance of Sixes tries to stifle.

A sign of growth for Sixes is the transformation of their fearful self-doubt to audacious self-confidence. When this transformation takes place, Sixes become a source of grounded faith rooted in their tenacious fortitude.

THE WAY HOME FOR TYPE SEVEN:
Rest in Silence

Intelligence Center	Head/Mind/Thinking
Harmony Triad	Idealist
Dominant Affect Group	Frustration
Prayer Posture	Silence
Prayer Intention	Rest

Probably the most frequently mistyped within the Enneagram's Intelligence Centers, people dominant in type Seven can resemble the Heart Center due to their winsome effervescence and social warmth. This is one of the ways Sevens avoid pressing into the complex space that is their inner life, specifically as it relates to their thoughts.

Sevens are actually so disconnected from their heart that they imagine it to be a quicksand of pain from which they will never be free. To avoid stepping into the quicksand, they fill life with all manner of fun.

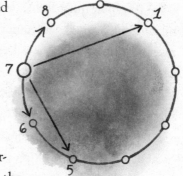

Because Sevens generously share their imaginative access to opportunity, they frequently emerge as the moving force in their social circles, communities, or families—we almost always love being around them. But our joyful attention often serves to fortify the lie they fall into: "I am what I have." Sevens looks for security outside of themselves: in people, places, things, and experiences. "Having" these things is their illusory freedom.

Perpetual idealists in their perceptions of freedom, Sevens are sometimes thought to lack the ability to follow through with their initiatives. However, this may in fact be more of a resistance to feeling forced to bring closure—which limits freedom and feels like dying to the Seven.

True freedom calls for Sevens to arrest their chronic escapism by learning to *rest in silence*. The journey home requires truthfulness in facing what, for many Sevens, is the undramatic pain of the ordinary; it requires them to welcome the emptiness they are afraid awaits them in silence.

For Sevens who are always in pursuit of options and opportunities, *silence* seems dull and repressive. Turning down the inner chatter that keeps them distracted from their own pain triggers the frustration they incessantly struggle with. As a Dominant Affect Group Frustration type, Sevens find that *rest* allows them to take a break from the exasperation of feeling like they never have enough of what brings them pleasure.

The prayer intention of the Seven is *rest*. Rest from the drive to imagine and inspire, rest from the pressure to keep moving forward, rest from the compulsion to live "free."

For Sevens, learning to *rest in silence* is the first step toward clarity in contemplation. When Sevens do make room in their minds for silence, it is often filled with imaginative ideas and dreamy visions of all the bliss they yet anticipate. The pleasure they explore in their head adds to the frustration that no experience could ever match their idealized fantasy experience. Thus, making space to cease the constant mental activity brings inner refreshment for rootedness in the present moment.

Since contemplative practice is a way of practicing dying to self, Sevens typically avoid contemplative prayer—all the more illuminating their need for it. For Sevens to harness the gifts of contemplative spirituality, they must learn to rest in silence, dialing back their mental preoccupations of what's next. Their resistance to silence is the first invitation for Sevens to face their own unconscious pain, the very thing they are running from in their efforts to create activity all around themselves.

THE WAY HOME FOR TYPE EIGHT:
Consent to Stillness

Intelligence Center	Body/Gut/Instinctive
Harmony Triad	Relationist
Dominant Affect Group	Rejection
Prayer Posture	Stillness
Prayer Intention	Consent

Those dominant in type Eight are the most engaged with their bodies, often using the force of presence to exert control or dominate their environments.

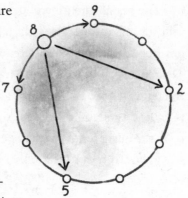

Coming home for an Eight means accepting the body as a gift—an integral part of essence expressed through the instincts— while at the same time not allowing the body to drive them to the end of their limits in the ways they continually exhaust themselves.

The lie Eights tend to believe—"I am what I do"—supports the addiction to frenetic activity that often lands them in trouble.

As one of the Harmony Triads' Relationist types, Eights tend to create pain in most of their relationships by overdoing everything, being too much for people to handle. Their aggressive and assertive social style can be dangerous—especially if they don't stop to make room for *stillness*. Often they end up wreaking the same havoc on themselves that they've levied on the world around them.

If the invitation for the Eight is to emphasize stillness as their prayer posture, the intention is to *consent*. Consent may be the toughest for the Eight because it relates to the fear of not being in control. Consent challenges the Eight to move from holding power to consciously letting it go.

Eights are among the Rejection Dominant Affect Group, using their powerful presence to move against the nurturing they need (and are frequently incapable of offering themselves in constructive or healthy ways) as a way of preemptively forcing rejection or, conversely, building trust.

Those dominant in type Eight need to learn to *consent to stillness* by deliberate choice, not through passive acquiescence or compliant submissiveness. Offering themselves to stillness may be frustrating at first. Their inability to be still or merely stop to be present may confront their compulsive desire to control the way they pray. Their initial inability to patiently practice stillness also may bring forward self-directed anger and resentment for not being able to do it effectively and efficiently.

THE WAY HOME FOR TYPE
NINE: Engaging Stillness

Intelligence Center	Body/Gut/Instinctive
Harmony Triad	Pragmatist
Dominant Affect Group	Attachment
Prayer Posture	Stillness
Prayer Intention	Engage

Those dominant in type Nine are among the three Anchor Points (connected by the only equilateral triangle in the center of the Enneagram); as a result, they are the most disconnected from their Intelligence Center, in their case, their gut or their body.

For a Nine coming home means engaging their own body, but not overidentifying with the activity tied to the instincts of their body (the compulsion to mediate or peace-build as a way of keeping their minds calm and their hearts protected). Nines tend to attach to relationships or scenarios that need mediation and reconciliation so they don't have to face their own unreconciled inner self.

Threes, Sixes, and Nines are the Attachment types of the Dominant Affect Groups. Nines specifically attach to both the protective and nurturing energy of their caregiver(s), which leads to addictive pseudo-self-nurturing and pseudo-self-protection, manifested in the way they lethargically check out of life. The spiritual growth invitation for the Nine is to move from this natural tendency to an attentive *stillness* in their prayer practice.

Because Nines are so capable of reconciling their exterior world, they withdraw into autonomy for self-nurturing and self-protection. But withdrawing isn't enough; they need to *engage* the stillness, learning how to show up when they'd rather check out.

So the invitation for the Nine is to *engage stillness*. Actively participating in intentional stillness will bring the Nine's practice an alertness that animates their own inner energies. Of course, physical stillness typically comes easily for Nines—they can turn off their thoughts, put aside their feelings, and just be. But *engaging* stillness energizes the core instincts and integration of the Nine's wholeness.

By engaging stillness, Nines learn to attach to their own bodies, thus awakening their capacity to engage all the aspects of life they've otherwise set aside. Stillness then is a gift helping Nines get back in touch with their own needs: genuine self-nurture and self-protection. Then the active energy of the love they've accessed by engaging stillness drives them to embody the harmonious world they hope to live in.

As we have seen, knowing our type's particular posture and intention is crucial, but *contemplative* prayer practices are what help us wake up from our illusions. If you're new to contemplative prayer, we'll examine a few practices in the final chapter to help you get started.

An Invitation *to* Inner Work

Getting Started in the Contemplative Journey

Now that you've identified your unique path to spiritual growth by way of your type-specific prayer posture and intention, you may wonder how to begin orienting yourself toward solitude, silence, or stillness. Let me offer some tangible prayer practices as an on-ramp to the historic Christian contemplative tradition. Following are a few practices I've found particularly helpful.

CENTERING PRAYER:
Praying with the Feeling Center

One of the most accessible contemplative prayer practices within the historic Christian faith tradition is Centering Prayer, which is why I recommend it as a place to begin putting this new knowledge into practice. Though it's not easy, it's a simple way to start nurturing contemplative spirituality. There are even Centering Prayer groups all over the world to help people get started in their practice and stay committed to it.

Centering Prayer is a nonconceptual prayer practice rooted in the Christian tradition but not formalized into a method until the 1970s by three Trappist monks: Fathers Basil Pennington, William Meninger, and Thomas Keating. Centering Prayer is a silent prayer that prepares its practitioner to receive the gift of loving presence in contemplative prayer. Centering Prayer complements and supports other forms of prayer by facilitating rest in God. It offers a way to grow in intimacy with God, moving beyond conversation to communion.

The method is simple:

1. Sit in an upright, attentive posture that allows for an erect spine and open heart. Place your hands on your lap.
2. Gently close your eyes and bring to mind a word, image, or breath as your symbol to consent to the presence and action of God within you. Your sacred symbol is intended to be the same every time you pray. It helps to ground you in the present moment, allowing you to give your undivided, loving, yielded attention to God. You may want to choose a name for God or a characteristic of God, such as Love, Peace, etc.
3. Silently, with eyes closed, recall your sacred symbol to begin your prayer. As you notice your thoughts, gently return to your sacred symbol. Do this as many times as you notice your thoughts. Don't forget, this is not about "getting it right"; there's no judgment in this practice.
4. When your prayer period is over, transition slowly from your prayer practice to your active life.

It's recommended that you practice Centering Prayer twice a day for twenty minutes each time. It's also recommended that you practice Centering Prayer for six months before giving up or determining it's not for you—it often can take that long (actually much longer for many of us) for the fruit of this prayer to blossom.

Centering Prayer is one of many contemplative prayer practices that is easily aligned with each specific Enneagram type, but even more so, it may be among the most effective in confronting the root addictions of each of the Enneagram's Intelligence Centers.

Aligning one's Intelligence Center (head, heart, body) with an interior posture (solitude, silence, stillness) allows for deep transformation to take place.

For those in the Head Center, Centering Prayer is an invitation to inner silence. The silence of God as a divine language may be something head people can agree with conceptually but find difficult to experience. Centering Prayer allows head people to arrest their mental obsessions and cultivate quiet to achieve a grounded peace.

For those in the Feeling Center, Centering Prayer is an invitation to inner solitude. By dialing down compulsions for connection and comparison, inner solitude enables heart people to face themselves in relationship to God. It allows for a deep experience of being loved, thereby helping heart people find their inner source of love for the world.

For those in the instinctive Body Center, Centering Prayer is an invitation to inner stillness—stopping and ceasing, resting in God. Centering Prayer slows down the initiating energy that drives gut people, creating a sacred pause that nurtures accountable action.

THE EXAMEN:
Praying with the Head Center

One of my favorite contemplative practices is the Ignatian prayer of Examen. The practice emerged from St. Ignatius of Loyola's *Spiritual Exercises* as a prayer to awaken consciousness to God's ever-present nearness (as opposed to prayers of confession and repentance used to clear one's conscience).

Essentially the practice is a journey through five movements that foster a reflective stance, helping us find God's movement toward us in very ordinary experiences:

1. We begin with a prayer for enlightenment. The Examen begins by recognizing God is with us as we are, always present and always loving.

2. Next we move into reflective thanksgiving. When we open our hearts to gratitude, we open our souls to hearing from God.

3. At this point we take a practical survey of the day. The heart of the Examen uses memory to explore the day searching for a *consolation*—a moment, memory, or experience in which we felt God moving toward us or in us. Our consolation can be something as mundane as our first cup of hot coffee in the morning, something as sweet as an interaction with a child we love, or something as profound as a personal eruption of grace (such as receiving forgiveness from a friend, noticing growth in our faith journey, or realizing in a deep way that we are loved). Whatever the consolation is, once it is discerned we allow ourselves to be held by it, listening to what God may be trying to say to us through it. This step of the prayer also invites us to find the courage to search for a *desolation*—a moment, attitude, or experience in our day in which we found ourselves moving away from God's love and presence. Perhaps it's those voices in our head—shame, guilt, doubt, regret, disappointment, or fear—that we mistake for the voice of Love. The person who hurt us isn't the desolation, but rather the resentment we might feel toward that person; the family member who constantly annoys us isn't the desolation, but rather our impatience with them; the painful memory we've tried so hard to forget isn't the desolation, but rather our inability to receive healing for it. Whatever the desolation is, we acknowledge it as an invitation to grace so as not to be overcome or overwhelmed by it.

4. After identifying our consolation and desolation, we express contrition or sorrow. Once we've found the honesty to face our desolation, we pray with it. For some of us the prayer is one of remorse or contrition. For others it may be heartfelt repentance, sorrow, lament, or just an appeal for help to let it go. This step of the prayer is a time to rest in the grace that God is bigger than our biggest problems, failures, hurts, or concerns.

5. Finally, we close with hopeful resolution for the future. We turn to the coming gift of a new morning, when the sunrise will be a symbolic baptism of a new day to be in the presence of a loving God, new opportunities to practice gratitude, new consolations and desolations, and new invitations to deeper growth.

I like how the Jesuit priest Father Dennis Hamm puts it. In his classic article "Rummaging for God: Praying Backwards through your Day,"[1] he compares using memory in prayer to searching for something, much like we rummage through a desk drawer, purse, or backpack to find our keys—using our hands to "see" something that we recognize once we find it because we're already familiar with it. This is the gift of the Examen, appealing to nontypical senses to find something or hear something that we know we've already found or heard but may have lost or forgotten along the way.

THE WELCOMING PRAYER:
Praying with the Instinctive Body Center

Just about every one of us carries some of our guilt or shame, anxiety or distress, and frustration or anger in our bodies. If you simply pause for a moment, close your eyes, find your breath (even just a few slow, deep, and deliberate breaths begin to restore your nervous system), and scan your body for any uncomfortable sensations, I'm certain you'll notice something.

It may be the "butterflies" or the irritation in your stomach. Perhaps it's the tightness in your chest when you concentrate on your breathing. Maybe it's the knots in your upper back and shoulders. Sometimes it's the tension at the base of your neck. Many people hardly notice that their jaw aches a bit from grinding their teeth while sleeping. Others may feel a little pressure in their temples or they've learned to live with temporary tension headaches. More often than not, these somatic discomforts are trying to get our attention. And I believe most of them can be directly tied to the Basic Fears or the most accessible emotion of the Intelligence Center of our Enneagram type.

I know for myself that a knot colonizes the space right behind the bottom of my right shoulder blade. When I stop to recognize it and listen to what it's trying to tell me, I usually can discern that it shows up when I feel frustrated or angry about not being in control of a situation.

The Welcoming Prayer helps us pray with these somatic flare-ups in our bodies. It is a method of actively letting go of thoughts and feelings that support the compulsions and addictions of the Basic Fears and Childhood Wounds that keep each Enneagram type's Fixation and Passion looped together.

Developed by Mary Mrozowski, one of the founders of Contemplative Outreach, the Welcoming Prayer invites God to dismantle the emotional programs for happiness to which we've attached ourselves and to help heal the emotional wounds we've stored in our bodies.

The method of the Welcoming Prayer includes noticing your feelings, emotions, and thoughts, as well as the sensations in your body, welcoming them, and then letting them go.

When you have an overly emotional experience in daily life, take a moment to be still and silent and follow these steps:

1. Focus on, feel, and sink into the feelings, emotions, thoughts, sensations, and commentaries in your body. Find your tension, tightness, soreness, or pressure and acknowledge it.
2. Welcome God into the feelings, emotions, thoughts, sensations, or commentaries in your body. Pray with your somatic discomfort; ask what it is telling you about your fear or your sense of being out of control or your lack of trust or your anxiety.
3. When the intensity of the body sensation or emotion begins to subside, let go by repeating the following sentences: "I let go of the desire for security/affection/control." "I let go of the desire to change this feeling/sensation." As you pray, recognize that God is with you.

The purpose of the Welcoming Prayer is to deepen your relationship with God by giving you an opportunity to consent to God's healing presence and action in the ordinary activities of daily life, thereby equipping you to respond skillfully to life's circumstances rather than react to them out of fear, shame, or frustration.

FINDING NEW WAYS TO COME HOME

If you commit to these practices, you'll find they soon become established disciplines. And as with any practice, you'll find the effects strengthen over time. Consistent contemplative prayer, used together with the Enneagram in a sort of cross-training technique, creates strong spiritual muscles that bear out transformation in all areas of life.

We notice a deeper sense of groundedness in all three of our centers. Our conscious mind becomes a quiet place of clarity that isn't overactive and constantly distracted. The powerful emotions of our subconscious are less reactive and can be trusted as a place to practice discernment. And the unconscious energy we carry in our body loosens its somatic grasp.

There is no better remedy for the addictions that keep us asleep than contemplative practice.

One autumn, I registered for a silent Ignatian retreat led by my spiritual director Father Larry Gillick. I hadn't been to visit him for a while, and it was catching up to me. I knew I was long overdue for spiritual guidance, but I thought spending a whole weekend on a group retreat would be an adequate substitute for a private spiritual direction session.

I signed up late, just a few days before the retreat was to begin, and didn't want to mention it to Father Gillick. Besides, I was still feeling guilty for slacking, so I hoped I could slip in and out without him noticing me. However, the night before the retreat, his secretary called. "Hi, Chris, Father Gillick noticed your name listed for this weekend's retreat and was wondering if you wouldn't mind driving him from his home to the monastery and back."

No longer able to hide from Father Gillick, I figured the ninety-minute drive to and from the monastery could count as some make-up spiritual direction sessions, so I agreed.

That Friday afternoon I arrived at the community house where he lived and helped him load his weekend bag into my car. As we pulled out of the driveway, my old-school GPS device (fastened to the inside of my windshield with a clear plastic suction cup) blurted out, "In 500 feet, turn right!"

A little startled, Father Gillick responded, "What's that?"

"It's my GPS. It'll help us find our way to the monastery," I said.

"Oh, this will be interesting," he replied. Which I thought was an intriguing response.

With that, we continued on our way. What was *really* interesting were the four or five times that Father Gillick suggested alternate routing from what my GPS suggested. He'd comment, "Don't turn here; keep going. I know a faster way." Which of course was helpful but caught me off guard, given that his blindness prevented him from seeing where we were each time he offered alternatives to the GPS.

Sure enough, he did get us there about ten minutes earlier than the GPS originally predicted.

Pretty amazing.

The retreat was just what I needed. Father Gillick's ability to demystify mysticism is undeniably remarkable. Years later I continue to learn from those forty-eight hours of guided silence and prayer.

After packing the car to go home, Father Gillick said, "Hey, no need to turn that GPS on; I'll direct you back."

Now, here's the thing: the Benedictine monastery is less than eighty miles from the city and is more or less a straight drive on just a few main streets and country roads—but I was seriously wondering how this was going to work out.

I knew the first few turns and got started. When Father Gillick rolled down the passenger side window, I offered, "If you're getting warm, I can turn the air conditioner on."

"No thanks. There are some train tracks up here, and I love to hear the sound of train cars passing by," he said.

Just at that moment, I kid you not, a Union Pacific train came speeding alongside and passed our car. I couldn't believe it. How did he know?

About ten minutes later he said, "We should be coming up on a tractor factory soon. Could you describe to me what they have sitting on their lot today?" And sure enough, I looked ahead and there it was. Unbelievable.

Another fifteen or twenty miles down the road, Father Gillick said, "So anytime now we should be driving under a bridge. Take the next exit; I know a shortcut home." It was almost at the very moment the words came out of his mouth that we drove under that little bridge.

With gentle directions, he did in fact get us right back to his front door. I was in disbelief; it's hard to explain how surreal that drive home was.

When I got to our brown-brick townhouse, Phileena greeted me at the door. "How was the retreat?" she asked.

How was the retreat? I responded, "You mean, how was the ride home?" She stared at me in confusion, so I told her the story.

I often think about that eighty-minute drive as a metaphor for the spiritual journey. As we give ourselves to contemplative practice, aligning prayer postures with intentions to support our spiritual growth, something happens to us. We find *new ways* of coming home.

Sure, the normal route works just fine and the typical tools we appeal to will get the job done adequately, but *if* and *when* we do the inner work required to wake up, to integrate the disconnected bits of ourselves, to dismantle the mythology of our ego projection, and to really tell ourselves the truth about who we are, *then* the growth we hope for sets in.

The Enneagram is one of the most effective companions to contemplative practice, a sacred map giving us new ways of seeing what we've been unable to see and new ways of finding our way home.

Afterword

by Ryan O'Neal

When Chris first introduced my wife, Cayt, and me to the Enneagram in 2012, I was a bit skeptical but also intrigued. I was familiar with other personality "typing" systems, none of which ever resonated with me, but because of my great respect for Chris, I knew I should at least pay close attention to what he shared with us. I asked the natural (and probably narcissistic) first question most folks ask when hearing about the Enneagram for the first time: *How do I know what type I am?* Translation: "Tell me more about me!" (I'm type Nine, by the way.)

Chris went on to explain the three Intelligence Centers and patiently described all nine types, encouraging us to read more on our own about each of them. He told us, or maybe warned us, that we would recognize ourselves in whichever type description "hurt" the most. Not exactly a fun entry point to learning anything about oneself, but that is exactly what gave the Enneagram credibility in my eyes. It's not just about the wonderful strengths we all possess but, if it is a map to our True Selves as Chris so elegantly illustrates throughout *The Sacred Enneagram*, it is a brutally honest one that boldly shows us the rough terrain that lies ahead.

In the days after Chris introduced us to these nine intricate types, I began to see traces of the Enneagram in every one of my friendships and relationships. I couldn't escape it, and I couldn't get enough of it. It brought language to so many confusing aspects of my personality and those of the people I love. It facilitated transformational conversations between my wife and me, as we processed how our unique types interact in healthy and unhealthy ways. The Enneagram became a staggeringly beautiful tool for empathy in my life.

My growing interest in studying the Enneagram, paired with Chris's generosity and patience, resulted in taking several trips together. In the time we shared, he walked me through integration and disintegration patterns, the Harmony Triads, the real and/or perceived Childhood Wounds of each type, and his beautiful and soul-enriching application of contemplative prayer postures to the three Intelligence Centers. A songwriter by trade, I was even led to my current project: nine songs written for the nine Enneagram types.

As I dig deeper and deeper into each type, with the hope of honoring its unique qualities, strengths, and struggles, Chris has been an invaluable wealth of insight and inspiration. What a great privilege to be taken under the wing (Enneagram pun intended) of such an important voice for the Enneagram.

Though he is extraordinarily generous with his time, I like to think that Chris wrote this book as a manual for all of us who have endlessly called on him in our quest to better understand ourselves through the Enneagram. I am so grateful that his wisdom has now been distilled in one place. The pages of this book will be well worn as I continue my own inner work.

So I congratulate you, dear reader, for having picked up such an important and life-giving book. Whether you're an Enneagram novice or expert, you'll continue to unpack and digest its contents for a long,

long while and see a ripple effect for years to come. Your heart will grow more empathetic toward yourself and others, your relationships will reach richer depths, and I believe that you will find it easier and easier to see God's grace and care in the nine complex and endlessly beautiful Enneagram types which God so lovingly created.

Ryan O'Neal
Songwriter, Sleeping At Last

Acknowledgments

I think I now understand why the Enneagram has been an oral tradition for thousands of years. To try to limit its dynamic mystery and forceful beauty within the confines of the written page is quite a daunting task. My own attempt here to offer a simple snapshot of one of the Enneagram's many facets has only developed within me even more admiration and respect for those who have previously done this with such elegance. I hope this volume's contribution is a tangible symbol of the gratitude I have for all the great teachers and authors before me.

My gratitude for the support and assistance in seeing this book come together is extended here to a community who has lent me their best—their love, their insights, their time, and their solidarity.

MY TEACHERS

David Daniels, Marion Gilbert, Craig Greenfield, Russ Hudson, Michael Naylor, Peter O'Hanrahan, Helen Palmer, Father Richard Rohr, Renée Rosario, Terry Saracino, Gayle Scott, and N'Shama Sterling: Thank you for sharing the wealth of the riches of your abundance. Thank you for embodying the gift of your knowledge. Thank you for pointing us to a better world. I am indebted to you.

MY AGENT

Chris Ferebee: Thank you for your persistence in pressing me to write this book. Thank you for advising and guiding me through the murky waters of an industry I still can't make sense of. Thank you for your friendship. Your brotherhood is a treasure.

MY PUBLISHER

The Zondervan team—Robin Barnett, Bridgette Brooks, Greg Clouse, Tom Dean, Amanda Halash, Harmony Harkema, Alicia Kasen, Kait Lamphere, Carolyn McCready, David Morris, Joyce Ondersma, Paige Raabe, Lauren Schneider, Stephanie Smith, Estee Zandee, and the others who have worked on this project: Thank you for giving me a chance to work with your fabulous team. Thank you for including me in the canon of your collective publishing efforts.

MY EDITORS

Greg Clouse and Stephanie Smith: First to you, Steph, thank you for believing in the importance of this book. Thank you for pressing me to excellence, especially when I may have been difficult. Thank you for your determination to ensure the ideas were clear. You've been an absolute joy to work with and a cherished companion on this book's journey to completion. To you, Greg, thank you for seeing the possibilities in clumsy phrases and 210+ word "sentences." Thank you for the respect you brought in caring for these ideas. Thank you for helping carry me over the finish line when I was ready to give up.

MY ILLUSTRATOR

Elnora Turner: Thank you for the tastefully handcrafted illustrations that bring this book to life, and for your curiosity in making flat diagrams seem warm and inviting. Thank you for tolerating me through my ridiculous requests for revisions. I just might *make up* projects so we can continue to work together.

MY RESEARCHERS

Angela Griner and Stacy Griner: Thank you both for shaping the initiative to give people the ability to discern for themselves how each individual type can truly be a path to God. Your professionalism and academic acumen in service to spirituality is refreshing.

MY REVIEW READERS

Julie Abendroth, Brent Crampton, Nicole Jordan, Avon Manney, Rob O'Callaghan, Ryan O'Neal, Anahí Salazar, Victoria Rosales, and Ted Warin: Thank you for not laughing when I sent you 40 percent of this book assuming I had captured everything I hoped to communicate. Thank you for your honesty, pushing back on unfinished ideas and underdeveloped concepts. Thank you for seeing what this could be and pressing me toward what it has become.

MY COMMUNITY

Gravity, a Center for Contemplative Activism—Cesia Gonzalez, Ying Guo, Mona Haydar, Melanie Kim, Vera Leung, Nikole Lim, George Mekhail, Richard Rohr, and Anahí Salazar: Thank you for granting me time in the rhythm and flow of my regular responsibilities to prioritize the writing of this book. Thank you for supporting my vocational fidelity. Thank you for investing in the kind of world we all hope to live in. Each of you are luminaries and have my deepest respect.

MY PARTNER

Phileena: You are my life. You are my love. Thank you for everything, absolutely everything.

Appendix 1

EnneaGlossary

Anchor Points – Types Three, Six, and Nine (also sometimes called the Revolutionary Types) are the midpoints or anchors of the Intelligence Center in which they are located.

Basic Desire – Each person's Basic Desire is the unique way they want to get home to their True Self, or the ego's yearning to return to its essence. The Basic Desire expresses itself as the core motivation behind a person's behavior, driving their actions in day-to-day life.

Basic Fear – Each Enneagram type has an underlying fear or dread that its Basic Desire will never be truly satisfied. Each type's Basic Fear emerges as a person begins to believe that reconnecting with the essence of the True Self is impossible.

Childhood Wound(s) – The lasting effect that is formed within a person when they feel they are not being loved perfectly, or a person's inability to receive love perfectly. The devastating way that the ego internalizes the impression of the caregiver's shadow (their unexamined and often unhealthy traits or behaviors). It's important to note the Enneagram's Childhood Wound can be a perceived or real experience.

Conscious Mind – The ego's layer of awareness that supports its ability to perceive itself through cognition, emotion, and instinct.

Contemplation – An intentional, introspective state of letting go and resting in God.

Dominant Affect Groups – The grouping of Enneagram types correlated to their object relations, or the theory of how one's sense of self emerges from mirroring in early childhood. These three groups include a triad of Enneagram types around frustration (types One, Four, and Seven), rejection (types Two, Five, and Eight), and attachment (types Thee, Six, and Nine) in relation to the nurturing and/or protective energy of one's caregiver(s).

Ego – One's identity construct, or how the self perceives the self.

False Self – The functioning pseudo-self that perpetuates self-destructive patterns, behaviors, and tendencies based on its addictions to power and control, affection and esteem, or security and survival.

Fixations – The Enneagram's nine type-specific ways the uncentered mind rationalizes the uncentered behavior of the Passion. If the Holy Ideas of each type demonstrate a mind fully awake and at peace, the Fixations demonstrate a mind asleep and stuck in illusions of self.

Harmony Triads – The three clusters of Enneagram types that display how the types function within the world, specifically through relationships (types Two, Five, and Eight), through idealism (types One, Four, and Seven), or through pragmatism (types Three, Six, and Nine). The Harmony Triads display how these three groups respond differently to relationships and obstacles in life.

Holy Ideas – The unique state of mental well-being, specific to each of the nine types, in which the mind is centered and connected with the True Self. The Holy Ideas are the fruit of each type when the mind is at peace, and stand in direct contrast to the Enneagram's Fixations, in which the mind is uncentered and disconnected from the True Self.

Inner Critic – The disapproving internal dialogue embedded in the subconscious that condemns the ego for its imperfections. The inner critic condemns the ego through messages of disappointment, doubt, guilt, regret, or shame, which are often mistaken as God's voice. Often considered part of the superego.

Inner Work – The practice of integrating self-awareness into action toward personal growth. These efforts are largely supported by contemplative practices.

Intelligence Centers – The Enneagram's three innate modes of perceiving reality: the head (rational faculties, thoughts, mindfulness); the heart (emotional intelligence, feelings, inner stability); and the body (gut feelings, instincts, intuition). Every Enneagram type has a dominant center of intelligence that it uses to bring clarity to self-awareness.

Intention – A prayerful concentration on the hoped-for outcome of contemplative practice; outlined in this book as it relates to the Enneagram as consent, engagement, or rest.

Non-dualism or Non-duality – The nonjudging awareness of the intrinsic oneness of all truth, resisting the reductionism that highlights the parts of a whole. An inner ability to reject classification, categorization, and compartmentalization; the conscious capacity to allow competing conclusions to coexist.

Passions – The Enneagram's nine type-specific emotional states of a heart disconnected from its True Self. The Passions emerge as the heart indulges the Basic Fear that it will never return to its essence and therefore seeks out coping mechanisms that ultimately compound each type's state of emotional imbalance. The Passions are the inverse of the Enneagram's Virtues, which are the emotional states of a centered heart at rest in the True Self.

Prayer Posture – The contemplative stances of solitude, silence, and stillness that hold a prayer intention.

Shadow – The unexamined or unconscious part of the ego where many of its (oftentimes perceived to be largely negative) traits are stored. Often mistaken for the False Self.

Subconscious – Influencing all aspects of our mental state, the layer of the ego's state of awareness entrenched in the feelings. Though incognizant of its subconscious, the ego is dependent on it for emotional intelligence that can't always be rationally explained or justified.

True Self – The integrated authentic self. Who each person is created and called to be when the heart is centered and the mind is at peace. One's essence or Essential Self.

Unconscious – The most expansive layer of the ego's state of awareness, including intuitive self-preservation instincts that go largely unregulated but are necessary for functioning (for example, blinking, metabolizing food, and breathing are unconscious functions of the body that are required for survival).

Virtue – Like the nine fruits of the Spirit, the Virtues are the Enneagram's nine type-specific gifts of a centered heart that is present, nonreactive, and at rest in the True Self. The inverse of the Virtues are the Passions.

Appendix 2

A Mistyping Chart for Every Enneagram Type Combination

I am grateful to the good people at pstypes.blogspot.com who granted permission to include these mistyping charts as an appendix. What's helpful about these columns of characteristics commonly associated with types is how they help navigate the nuanced variations of personality that sometimes lead to confusion or uncertainty of type.

ONE AND TWO

Mistyping frequency: sometimes (usually between Ones with a Two wing and Twos with a One wing).

One	Two
Impersonal	Personal
Autonomous	Merging
Criticizes	Compliments
Focused on principles	Focused on people
Emotionally restrained	Emotionally expressive
Logical	Loving
Reserved	Warm
Wants to be right	Wants to be loved

ONE AND THREE

Mistyping frequency: sometimes (usually Threes mistype as Ones).

One	Three
Idealistic	Pragmatic
Focuses on principles	Focuses on goals
Rigid	Highly adaptable
Irritable	Masked feelings
Angry	Arrogant
Indignation	Hostility
Suppression of feelings	Detachment from feelings
Self-righteous	Charming
Perfection	Desirability
Focuses on means	Focuses on ends

ONE AND FOUR

Mistyping frequency: rarely (usually unhealthy Ones mistype as Fours).

One	Four
Focuses on duties	Focuses on feelings
Self-denying	Self-indulgent
Pushes people	Withdraws from people
Disciplined	Whimsical
Constant	Changeable
Principled	Self-centered
Emotionally constrained	Emotionally expressive
Judgmental	Empathetic

ONE AND FIVE

Mistyping frequency: sometimes (Fives with a Six wing and Ones can resemble each other).

One	Five
Action	Thought
Certain	Uncertain
Convinces people	Disturbs people
Practical	Impractical
Rigid	Playful
Correct	Ingenious
Judgmental	Nonjudgmental
Discerning	Confuse
Controlling	Withdrawn
Involved	Detached
Realistic	Imaginative
Deductive logic	Inductive logic
Follows rules	Questions rules
Perfection	Discovery
Moralist	Iconoclast

ONE AND SIX

Mistyping frequency: rarely (Sixes with a Five wing can resemble Ones).

One	Six
Self-confident	Self-doubting
Decisive	Indecisive
Certain	Ambivalent
Contained	Reactive
Angry	Anxious
Indignant of others	Suspicious of others
Controlled	Temperamental
Seeks perfection	Seeks security
Independent	Affiliative
Becomes an authority	Looks to authority

ONE AND SEVEN

Mistyping frequency: very rarely (unhealthy Sevens mistype as Ones).

One	Seven
Pessimistic	Optimistic
Planned	Spontaneous
Self-conscious	Nonchalant
Knows their purpose	Intuits their purpose
Methodical	Scattered
Diligent	Easily distracted
Rather close-minded	Very open-minded
Work	Play
Dislikes changes	Wants changes
Mature	Childlike
Duty	Fun
Frugal	Spendthrift
Restrained	Uninhibited

ONE AND EIGHT

Mistyping frequency: **often** (generally Ones mistype as Eights).

One	Eight
The right way	"My way"
Convinces	Imposes
Focuses on morality	Focuses on power
Abstract	Visceral
Objective	Subjective
Concern for humanity	Concern for "their people"
Ashamed of their anger	Proud of their anger
Moral justice	Revenge
Cerebral	Physical
Moderated	Openly aggressive
Reserved	Expansive
Refined	Crude
Formal	Informal

ONE AND NINE

Mistyping frequency: **often** (usually between Ones with a Nine wing and Nines with a One wing).

One	Nine
Driven	Relaxed
Focuses on principles	Focuses on harmony
Takes on conflict	Avoids conflict
Works too much	Loves a break
Moody	Anxious
Fights for beliefs	Hides beliefs
Tense	Laid-back
Assertive	Withdrawn
Critical	Accepting
Persuades	Mediates
Diligent	Unmotivated

TWO AND THREE

Mistyping frequency: sometimes (usually between Twos with a Three wing and Threes with a Two wing).

Two	Three
Gives attention	Grabs attention
Seeks intimacy	Afraid of intimacy
Helps others	Impresses others
Emotional	Composed
Selfless	Selfish
Gets aggressive	Becomes detached
People	Goals
Sentimental	Ambitious
Be kind	Be successful
Romantic	Pragmatic

TWO AND FOUR

Mistyping frequency: sometimes (due to their emotionality).

Two	Four
Engaging	Withdrawn
Rescues	Wants to be rescued
Focuses on others	Focuses on self
Unaware of self	Introspective
Altruist	Individualist
Understanding	Misunderstood
Extroverted	Introverted
Positive	Negative
Feels superior	Feels inferior
Loving	Ambivalent

TWO AND FIVE

Mistyping frequency: very rarely (sexual Fives can be mistyped as Twos by others).

Two	Five
Emotional	Detached
Warm	Cold
People-oriented	Loner
Team-player	Individualist
Compassionate	Analytical
Sentimental	Cerebral
Empathizes	Intellectualizes
Helps	Withdraws
Seeks others	Afraid of others
Passionate	Cynical
Social	Unsocial

TWO AND SIX

Mistyping frequency: **often** (usually Sixes mistype as Twos).

Two	Six
Seeks love	Seeks support
Loving and helpful	Playful and silly
Sure of self	Unsure
Needs merging	Wants independence
Manipulative	Reactive
Positive feelings	Ambivalent
Becomes authority	Looks to authority
Makes others dependent	Becomes dependent
Self-assured	Self-doubting

TWO AND SEVEN

Mistyping frequency: **often** (usually Sevens mistype as Twos).

Two	Seven
Emotionally stable	Emotionally volatile
Seeks intimacy	Seeks adventure
Focuses on people	Focuses on enjoyment
Helps others	Helps self
Wants merging	Wants freedom
Possessive	Detached
Sentimental	Cerebral
Clingy	Lets go
Wants closeness	Wants company
Relationships	Activities
Considerate	Can be caustic
Keeps promises	Forgets promises
Kind humor	Abrasive humor

TWO AND EIGHT

Mistyping frequency: sometimes (usually Two men mistype as Eights).

Two	Eight
Dominates to help	Dominates for power
Manipulation	Open conflict
Hides anger	Shows anger
Indirect hints	Direct speaking
Dramatizes	Intimidates
Vulnerable	Tough
Others-focused	Self-focused
Wants appreciation	Wants authority

TWO AND NINE

Mistyping frequency: sometimes (usually Nine women mistype as Twos).

Two	Nine
Expecting	Accepting
Reads others	Idealizes others
Demanding	Accommodating
Self-important	Self-effacing
Expresses displeasure	Hides displeasure
Controlling	Easygoing
Helping	Comforting
Focused	Unfocused
Strong-willed	Nonassertive
Engaged	Disengaged
Involved	Withdrawn

THREE AND FOUR

Mistyping frequency: sometimes (generally Threes with a Four wing mistype as Fours with a Three wing).

Three	Four
Focuses on performance	Focuses on feelings
Self-disciplined	Self-indulging
Success-oriented	Introspective
Detached	Emotional
Socially confident	Socially unconfident
Adaptable	Different
Be impressive	Be themselves
Minimizes suffering	Dramatizes suffering
Positive self-image	Negative self-image

THREE AND FIVE

Mistyping frequency: sometimes (almost always Threes mistype as Fives).

Three	Five
Seeks recognition	Seeks knowledge
Goal-oriented	Process-oriented
Competitive	Withdrawn
Self-promoting	Secretive
Pragmatic	Impractical
Highly efficient	Curiously wandering
Socially competent	Socially awkward
Well-groomed	Image-unaware
Cares what others think	Ignores people's opinions
Admirable	Eccentric
Social standards	Social isolation

THREE AND SIX

Mistyping frequency: rarely (stressed out Sixes somewhat resemble Threes).

Three	Six
Wants the spotlight	Avoids the spotlight
Success	Security
Impressive	Dependable
Composed	Nervous
Admirably smooth	Endearingly awkward
Confident appearance	Visible insecurity
Emotionally reserved	Emotionally intense
Cool	Reactive
Optimistic	Pessimistic

THREE AND SEVEN

Mistyping frequency: **often** (both are assertive types).

Three	Seven
Focuses on competition	Focuses on enjoyment
Be admired	Have fun
Success	Freedom
Inflated self-worth	Inflated plans and desires
Arrogant	Maniacal
Self-controlled	Impulsive
Focused	Scattered
Composed	Bubbly
Well-mannered	Rather ill-mannered
Tactful	Outspoken
Polished	Rough-edged
Serious	Playful
Moderate	Gluttonous

THREE AND EIGHT

Mistyping frequency: sometimes (usually Threes mistype as Eights).

Three	Eight
Social status	Material and sexual dominance
Seeks validation	Seeks power
Prestige	Control
Scared of failure	Stirred by failure
Adaptable	Forceful
Becomes devious	Becomes intimidating
Competitive	Combative
Concerned with image	Unconcerned with image
Smooth	Crude
Well-mannered	Defiant

THREE AND NINE

Mistyping frequency: rarely (stressed-out Threes can resemble Nines).

Three	Nine
Highly motivated	Relaxed
Focused	Unfocussed
Driven	Easygoing
Seeks attention	Avoids attention
Self-confident	Self-effacing
Ambitious	Disengaging
Active	Low-key
Surpasses others	Merges with others
Show-off	Withdrawn
Arrogant	Modest

FOUR AND FIVE

Mistyping frequency: **often** (usually between Fives with a Four Wing and Fours with a Five wing).

Four	Five
Artistic	Scientific
Emotionally expressive	Emotionally restrained
Subjective	Objective
Reactive	Aloof
Inner pain	Inner emptiness
Identifies with feelings	Detaches from feelings
Welcomes feelings	Bothered by feelings
Romantic	Cerebral
Self-revealing	Self-protective
Melancholic	Nihilistic

FOUR AND SIX

Mistyping frequency: sometimes (usually individualistic Sixes mistype as Fours).

Four	Six
Introverted	Ambiverted
Loner	Affiliative
Creator	Performer
Ignores tradition	Relates to tradition
Politically neutral	Politically inclined
Personal truth	Common values
Reclusive	Bonding
Seeks ideal love	Seeks security
Different and sensitive	Loyal and reliable
Fantasy-prone	Anxiety-prone

FOUR AND SEVEN

Mistyping frequency: rarely (Sevens with a Six wing might resemble Fours with a Three wing).

Four	Seven
Idealistic	Materialistic
Introverted	Extroverted
Moody	Jovial
Loner	Outgoing
Sensitive	Insensitive
Focuses on beauty	Focuses on novelty
Impractical	Practical
Prefers fantasy	Prefers reality
Precious	Practical
Melancholic	Gluttonous
Pessimistic	Optimistic
Indulges in pain	Flees from pain
Inhibited	Confident

FOUR AND EIGHT

Mistyping frequency: rarely (sexual Fours can resemble Eights).

Four	Eight
Soft	Tough
Melancholic	Pragmatic
Vulnerable	Strong
Indulges in fantasy	Takes action
Self-loathing	Self-confident
Expresses emotions	Represses emotions
Impractical	Practical
Refined	Rather coarse

FOUR AND NINE

Mistyping frequency: sometimes (both are withdrawn types).

Four	Nine
Intense	Disengaged
Idealizes fantasies	Idealizes reality
Negative	Positive
Explores pain	Denies pain
Identifies with emotions	Detaches from emotions
Pessimistic	Optimistic
Conflictual	Avoids conflict
Misfit	Merges with others
Dark side	Bright side
Authentic	Submissive
Moody	Easygoing

FIVE AND SIX

Mistyping frequency: sometimes (Sixes with a Five wing and self-preservation Fives tend to resemble each other).

Five	Six
Eccentric	Relates to tradition
Ignores rules	Considers rules
Nonlinear thinking	Linear thinking
Contests methods	Establishes methods
Impractical	Practical
Trusts their mind	Doubts their mind
Aloof	Reactive
Independent	Affiliative
Seeks knowledge	Seeks security
Schizoid	Paranoid
Detached	Engaged
Individualist	Group-oriented

FIVE AND SEVEN

Mistyping frequency: rarely (stressed-out Fives can act like Sevens).

Five	Seven
Introverted	Extroverted
Withdrawn	Outgoing
Focused	Scattered
Analytical	Syntactical
Dark vision	Optimistic vision
Obsessive	Superficial
Seeks knowledge	Seeks pleasure
Shy	Gregarious
Needs quiet	Needs stimulation
Stingy	Generous
Reserved	Expansive

FIVE AND EIGHT

Mistyping frequency: rarely (between self-confident Fives and intellectual Eights).

Five	Eight
Withdrawn	Confrontational
Cerebral	Instinctual
Prepares	Acts
Impractical	Pragmatic
Retreats from life	Demands of life
Feels powerless	Feels powerful
Abstract	Grounded
Restrained	Expansive
Somewhat absent	Powerful presence
Sensitive	Insensitive
Overwhelmed	Overwhelming
Reserved	Aggressive

FIVE AND NINE

Mistyping frequency: **very often** (many Nines mistype as Fives).

Five	Nine
Intense	Soft
Strong-minded	Easygoing
Argumentative	Comforting
Resistant	Receptive
Suspicious	Trusting
Focused	Diffuse
Penetrating	Unfocused
Theory	Fantasy
Particularities	Generalities
Pessimistic	Optimistic
High-strung	Peaceful
Disconnects from others	Merges with others
Defensive	Accommodating
Complexifies things	Simplifies things
Discriminating	Accepting
Detaches	Spaces out

SIX AND SEVEN

Mistyping frequency: sometimes (Sixes with a Seven wing and Sevens with a Six wing can resemble each other).

Six	Seven
Pessimistic	Optimistic
Self-doubting	Self-confident
Responsible	Forgetful
Seeks guidelines	Rejects guidelines
Aware of authority	Ignores authority
Committed	Flighty
Negative	Upbeat
Duty	Freedom
Worrying	Diverting

SIX AND NINE

Mistyping frequency: **often** (stressed-out Nines can resemble Sixes).

Six	Nine
Suspicious	Trusting
Agitated	Easygoing
Worrying	Unperturbed
Magnifies problems	Ignores problems
Vents feelings	Hides feelings
Reacts	Withdraws
Intolerant	Accepting
Negative	Positive
Engaged	Disengaged
Complicated	Uncomplicated
Irritable	Serene

SIX AND EIGHT

Mistyping frequency: sometimes (usually counterphobic Sixes think they are Eights).

Six	Eight
Reactive	Strategic
Anxious	Powerful
Unsure	Willful
Ambivalent	Certain
Self-doubting	Self-assured
Needs protection	Offers protection
Feels pressured	Pressures others
Irrational outbreaks	Lucid anger
Contradictory	Consistent
Gives in	Resists
Volatile	Grounded
Hesitant	Forceful

SEVEN AND EIGHT

Mistyping frequency: sometimes (usually Sevens with an Eight wing mistype as Eights).

Seven	Eight
Seeks variety	Seeks intensity
Wants freedom	Wants control
Nervous energy	Physical energy
Playful	Hardworking
Scattered	Focused
Irresponsible	Conscientious
Optimist	Realist
Have fun	Gain power
Egalitarian	Authoritarian
Tolerant	Vengeful

SEVEN AND NINE

Mistyping frequency: rarely (both are optimistic types).

Seven	Nine
Extroverted	Withdrawn
Exaggerated	Balanced
Seeks stimulation	Seeks peace
Hyperactive	Passive
Euphoric	Contented
Involved	Unresponsive
Self-centered	Others-centered
Assertive	Compliant
Loves variety	Likes routine

EIGHT AND NINE

Mistyping frequency: rarely (Eights with a Nine wing can resemble Nines with an Eight wing).

Eight	Nine
Assertive	Self-effacing
Aggressive	Peaceful
Imposes	Compromises
Starts conflict	Avoids conflict
Engaged	Disengaged
Controlling	Easygoing
Directs	Mediates
Shows anger	Denies anger
Wants intensity	Wants routine
Powerful	Soft

Bibliography *and* Recommended Reading

Almaas, A. H. *Facets of Unity: The Enneagram of Holy Ideas.* Boston: Shambhala Publications, 1998.

Anderson, Gary A. *Sin: A History.* New Haven, CT: Yale University, 2009.

Bakhtiar, Laleh. *Rumi's Original Sufi Enneagram.* Chicago: Institute of Traditional Psychology, 2013.

——————. *The Sufi Enneagram: Sign of the Presence of God (Wajhullah): The Secrets of the Symbol Unveiled.* Chicago: Institute of Traditional Psychology, 2013.

Baron, Renee, and Elizabeth Wagele. *The Enneagram Made Easy.* New York: HarperOne, 1994.

Bartlett, Carolyn. *The Enneagram Field Guide: Notes on Using the Enneagram in Counseling, Therapy and Personal Growth.* Fort Collins, CO: Nine Gates, 2003.

Bast, Mary R. *Buddhism and the Enneagram.* Lexington, KY: self-published, 2014.

Berghoef, Kacie, and Melanie Bell. *The Modern Enneagram: Discover Who You Are and Who You Can Be.* Berkeley, CA: Althea Press, 2017.

Bennett, J. G. *Enneagram Studies.* Newburyport, MA: Red Wheel Weiser, 1983.

——————. *The Great Human Problems: A Study Course (The Collected Works of J. G. Bennett).* CreateSpace Independent Publishing Platform, 2017.

Bessenecker, Scott. *The New Friars: The Emerging Movement Serving the World's Poor.* Downers Grove, IL: InterVarsity Press, 2006.

Bourgeault, Cynthia. *The Holy Trinity and the Law of Three: Discovering the Radical Truth at the Heart of Christianity.* Boston: Shambhala Publications, 2013.

——————. *The Heart of Centering Prayer: Nondual Christianity in Theory and Practice.* Boulder, CO: Shambhala Publications, 2016.

Chestnut, Beatrice. *The Complete Enneagram: 27 Paths to Greater Self-Knowledge.* Berkeley, CA: She Writes Press, 2013.

——————. *The Enneagram System's 27 Personality Subtypes.* Self-published.

——————. *The Nine Types of Leadership: Mastering the Art of People in the 21st Century Workplace.* Brentwood, TN: Post Hill Press, 2017.

Cron, Ian Morgan, and Suzanne Stabile. *The Road Back to You: An Enneagram Journey to Self-Discovery.* Downers Grove, IL: InterVarsity Press, 2016.

Daniels, David N., and Virginia A. Price. *The Essential Enneagram: The Definitive Personality Test and Self-Discovery Guide—Revised and Updated.* New York: HarperOne, 2009.

Defouw, Richard J. *The Enneagram in the Writings of Gurdjieff.* Indianapolis: Dog Ear, 2011.

Emperuer, James. *The Enneagram and Spiritual Direction: Nine Paths to Spiritual Guidance.* New York: Continuum, 1997.

Fernández Christlieb, Fátima. *Where on Earth Did the Enneagram Come From?* Ciudad de México: Editorial Pax México, 2016.

Ginn, Robert W. *A Beautiful Career.* Bloomington, IN: Xlibris, 2010.

Goldberg, Michael J. *Travels with Odysseus: Uncommon Wisdom from Homer's Odyssey.* Tempe, AZ: Circle's Island Press, 2005.

Griner, Angela, and Stacey Griner. *Enneagram and Spiritual Practice.* Orlando: Rollins College, 2007.

Gurdjieff, G. I. *The Herald of Coming Good.* Edmond, OK: Sure Fire, 1988.

——————. *Life Is Real Only Then, When "I Am": All and Everything.* New York: Penguin Arkana, 1991.

——————. *Meetings with Remarkable Men.* Mansfield Center, CT: Martino Publishing, 2010.

Haines, Seth. *Coming Clean: A Story of Faith.* Grand Rapids: Zondervan, 2015.

Heuertz, Phileena. *Pilgrimage of a Soul: Contemplative Spirituality for the Active Life.* Downers Grove, IL: InterVarsity Press, 2010.

Horsely, Mary. *The Enneagram for the Spirit: How to Make Peace with Your Personality and Understand Others.* Hauppauge, NY: Barron's Educational Series, 2005.

Hurley, Kathleen, and Theodore Dobson. *My Best Self: Using the Enneagram to Free the Soul.* New York: HarperOne, 1993.

Ichazo, Óscar. *Between Metaphysics and Protoanalysis: A Theory for Analyzing the Human Psyche.* New York: Arica Institute Press, 1982.

—————. *Interviews with Óscar Ichazo.* New York: Arica Institute Press, 1982.

Johnson, Robert A. *Inner Work: Using Dreams and Active Imagination for Personal Growth.* New York: HarperOne, 1991.

—————. *Owning Your Own Shadow: Understanding the Dark Side of the Psyche.* New York: HarperOne, 1986.

Keating, Thomas. *The Human Condition.* New York: Paulist Press, 1999.

Lapid-Bogda, Ginger. *Bringing Out the Best in Yourself at Work: How to Use the Enneagram System for Success.* New York: McGraw-Hill Education, 2004.

—————. *The Enneagram Development Guide: Human Condition.* Santa Monica, CA: Ginger Lapid-Bogda, 2010.

Madanes, Yechezkel, and Ruth Madanes. *Enneagram Meditation: Insights to Empower Your Soul.* Lexington, KY: Madanes School of Enneagram Coaching, 2012.

Maitri, Sandra. *The Enneagram of Passions and Virtues: Finding the Way Home.* New York: Penguin, 2005.

—————. Foreword to *The Spiritual Dimension of the Enneagram* by Geneen Roth. New York: Penguin Putnam, 2000.

Metz, Barbara, and John Burchill. *The Enneagram and Prayer: Discovering Our True Selves Before God.* Denville, NJ: Dimension Books, 1987.

Naranjo, Claudio. *Character and Neurosis: An Integrative View.* Nevada City, CA: Gateways/IDHHB Publishers, 1994.

—————. *Ennea-Type Structures: Self-Analysis for the Seeker.* Nevada City, CA: Gateways Books and Tapes, 1990.

————. *The Enneagram of Society: Healing the Soul to Heal the World.* Translated by Paul Barnes. Nevada City, CA: Gateways Books and Tapes, 2004.

Nouwen, Henri. "*Moving from Solitude to Community to Ministry,*" *Leadership Journal* 16, no. 2 (Spring 1995).

Ouspensky, P. D. *Conscience: The Search for Truth.* Sandpoint, ID: Morning Light Press, 2008.

————. *The Fourth Way.* New York: Vintage, 1971.

————. *In Search for the Miraculous.* New York: Harcourt, 1949.

Palmer, Helen. *The Enneagram in Love and Work.* New York: HarperOne, 1995.

————. *The Enneagram: Understanding Yourself and the Others in Your Life.* New York: HarperOne, 1988.

Riso, Don Richard. *Discovering Your Personality Type: The Enneagram Questionnaire.* New York: Houghton Mifflin, 1992.

Riso, Don Richard, and Russ Hudson. *Personality Types: Using the Enneagram for Self-Discovery.* New York: Houghton Mifflin, 1996.

————. *Understanding the Enneagram: The Practical Guide to Personality Types.* New York: Houghton Mifflin, 2000.

————. *The Wisdom of the Enneagram: The Complete Guide to Psychological and Spiritual Growth for the Nine Personality Types.* New York: Bantam, 1999.

Rohr, Richard, and Andreas Ebert. *Discovering the Enneagram: An Ancient Tool for a New Spiritual Journey.* Translated by Peter Heinegg. New York: Crossroad, 1990.

————. *The Enneagram: A Christian Perspective.* Translated by Peter Heinegg. New York: Crossroad, 2006.

Rohr, Richard et al. *Experiencing the Enneagram.* Translated by Peter Heinegg. New York: Crossroad, 1992.

Sherrill, A. J. *Enneagram and the Way of Jesus: Intersecting Personality Theory with Spiritual Practices and Biblical Narratives.* CreateSpace Independent Publishing Platform, 2016.

Silverstein, Shel. *The Giving Tree.* New York: Harper and Row/Harper Collins, 1964.

Speeth, Kathleen Riordan. Foreword to *The Gurdjieff Work* by Claudio Naranjo. New York: Penguin, 1989.

Sugden, Chris. *Seeking the Asian Face of Jesus: The Practice and Theology of Christian Social Witness in Indonesia and India 1974–1996*. Oxford, England: Regnum, 1997.

Thomson, Clarence. *Parables and the Enneagram*. Portland, OR: Metamorphous Press, 1996.

Tickle, Phyllis. *The Great Emergence: How Christianity Is Changing and Why*. Grand Rapids: Baker, 2008.

Tolle, Eckhart. *Guardians of Being: Spiritual Teachings from Our Dogs and Cats*. Novato, CA: New World Library, 2011.

Vancil, Marilyn. *Self to Lose—Self to Find: A Biblical Approach to the 9 Enneagram Types*. Enumclaw, WA: Redemption Press, 2016.

Wagner, Jerome. *The Enneagram Spectrum of Personality Styles: An Introductory Guide*. Evanston, IL: Enneagram Studies and Applications, 1996.

—————. *Nine Lenses on the World: The Enneagram Perspective*. Evanston, IL: Enneagram Studies and Applications, 2010.

Zuercher, Suzanne. *Enneagram Companions: Growing in Relationships and Spiritual Direction*. Self-published, 2000.

—————. *Enneagram Spirituality: From Compulsion to Contemplation*. Notre Dame, IN: Ave Maria Press, 1992.

—————. *Using the Enneagram in Prayer*. Notre Dame, IN: Ave Maria Press, 2000.

Endnotes

Chapter 1: The Question of Identity

1. Chris Sugden, *Seeking the Asian Face of Jesus: The Practice and Theology of Christian Social Witness in Indonesia and India 1974–1996* (Oxford: Regnum, 1997), 183.
2. Ibid.
3. Thomas Keating, *The Human Condition: Contemplation and Transformation* (New York: Paulist Press, 1999), 9–10.

Chapter 2: What Is the Enneagram?

1. Phileena Heuertz, *Pilgrimage of a Soul: Contemplative Spirituality for the Active Life* (Downers Grove, IL: InterVarsity Press, 2010), 19.
2. Samuel Bendeck Sotillos, introduction to *The Sufi Enneagram: The Secrets of the Symbol Unveiled* by Laleh Bakhtiar (Chicago: Institute of Traditional Psychology, 2013), xi.
3. Beatrice Chestnut, *The Nine Types of Leadership: Mastering the Art of People in the 21st Century Workplace* (Brentwood, TN: Post Hill Press, 2017), 24. [These ideas originally appeared in Michael J. Goldberg's *Travels with Odysseus: Uncommon Wisdom from Homer's Odyssey.*]
4. Richard Rohr and Andreas Ebert, *The Enneagram: A Christian Perspective* (New York: Crossroad, 2001), 8–14.
5. Kathleen Riordan Speeth, *The Gurdjieff Work* (New York: Jeremy P. Tarcher/Putnam, 1989), 5.
6. P. D. Ouspensky, *In Search of the Miraculous: Fragments of an Unknown Teaching* (New York: Harcourt, Brace and World, 1949), 294.

7. Speeth, *Gurdjieff Work*, 15.

8. Helen Palmer, *The Enneagram: Understanding Yourself and the Others in Your Life* (New York: HarperOne, 1988), 13–15.

9. Claudio Naranjo, *The Enneagram of Society: Healing the Soul to Heal the World* (Nevada City, Calif.: Gateways Books and Tapes, 2004), 33.

10. Sandra Maitri, *The Spiritual Dimension of the Enneagram: Nine Faces of the Soul* (New York: Jeremy P Tarcher/Putnam, 2000), 6.

Chapter 3: Paths of Integration, Disintegration, and Grace for the Journey

1. Elbert Hubbard, *The Note Book of Elbert Hubbard: Mottoes, Epigrams, Short Essays, Passages, Orphic Sayings and Preachments* (New York: Wm. B. Wise & Co., 1927), 12.

2. Claudio Naranjo, *The Enneagram of Society: Healing the Soul to Heal the World* (Nevada City, CA: Gateways Books and Tapes, 2004), 22.

3. Ibid.

4. Ibid., 23.

5. Ibid.

Chapter 4: Head, Heart, Body, and the Whole Self

1. Richard Rohr, "The Enneagram (Part 1): Overview of Enneagram Triads and Types," Richard Rohr's Daily Meditation, May 27, 2014. http://myemail.constantcontact.com/Richard-Rohr-s-Meditation-Overview-of-Enneagram-Triads-and-Types.html?soid=1103098668616&aid=N21lO8jiNnY.

2. Ibid.

3. Ibid.

4. Claudio Naranjo, *Character and Neurosis: An Integrative View* (Nevada City, CA: Gateways/IDHHB, 1994), 21.

Chapter 5: A Curated Color Wheel Summary of the Nine Types

1. All Childhood Wounds are taken from the EnneApp (created by Elan BenAmi, MA, LPC with material provided by Lori Ohlson, MA, LPC.).

2. Claudio Naranjo, *Character and Neurosis: An Integrative View* (Nevada City, CA: Gateways/IDHHB, 1994), 23.

Chapter 6: Relationists, Pragmatists, and Idealists

1. David Daniels, "Working with the Harmony Triads," *The Harmony Triads*, November 9, 2012. http://drdaviddaniels.com/the-Enneagram/the-harmony-triads/.
2. Ibid.
3. Ibid.
4. Ibid.
5. Cynthia Bourgeault, *The Heart of Centering Prayer: Nondual Christianity in Theory and Practice* (Boulder, CO: Shambhala Publications, 2016), 54. Emphasis added.
6. Don Richard Riso and Russ Hudson, *Understanding the Enneagram: The Practical Guide to Personality Types* (New York: Houghton Mifflin, 2000), 315–20.
7. Ibid., 317.
8. Noted in a lecture by Gayle Scott of the Enneagram Institute's Enneagram Professional Training Program in Burlingame, CA, July 28–August 3, 2014.
9. Riso and Hudson, *Understanding the Enneagram*, 316. Emphasis added.
10. Noted in a lecture by Gayle Scott of the Enneagram Institute's Enneagram Professional Training Program in Burlingame, CA, July 28–August 3, 2014.
11. Riso and Hudson, *Understanding the Enneagram*, 316–317. Emphasis added.
12. Noted in a lecture by Gayle Scott of the Enneagram Institute's Enneagram Professional Training Program in Burlingame, CA, July 28–August 3, 2014.

Chapter 7: The Unexpected Gifts of Solitude, Silence, and Stillness

1. Robert W. Ginn, *A Beautiful Career* (Bloomington, IN: Xlibris, 2010).
2. Drew Jackson, "The Contemplative Way as a Practice in Death," Gravity Reference. December 1, 2016. https://gravitycenter.com/life-found-dying/.
3. Ibid.
4. Eckhart Tolle, *Guardians of Being: Spiritual Teachings from Our Dogs and Cats* (Novato, CA: New World Library, 2011).

5. Phileena Heuertz, *Pilgrimage of a Soul: Contemplative Spirituality for the Active Life* (Downers Grove, IL: InterVarsity Press, 2010), 15.

6. Ibid., 186.

7. Thomas Keating, *The Human Condition: Contemplation and Transformation* (New York: Paulist Press, 1999), 13.

8. Scott Bessenecker, *The New Friars: The Emerging Movement Serving the World's Poor* (Downers Grove, IL: InterVarsity Press, 2006), 19.

9. Phyllis Tickle, *The Great Emergence: How Christianity Is Changing and Why* (Grand Rapids: Baker, 2008), 19–31.

Chapter 10: An Invitation to Inner Work

1. Dennis Hamm, SJ, "Rummaging for God: Praying Backwards through Your Day," *Ignatian Spirituality*, May 14, 1994. http://www.ignatianspirituality.com/ignatian-prayer/the-examen/rummaging-for-god-praying-backward-through-your-day.

THREE
FREE
SONGS

FROM *sleeping at last*

Inspired by the Enneagram
Intelligence Centers

SLEEPINGATLAST.COM/SACREDENNEAGRAM
PASSWORD: SACRED

The Free *Intelligence EP* is a prelude to Sleeping At Last's
Enneagram album, a collection of nine songs representing
each of the nine Enneagram types.

The Enneagram of Belonging

A Compassionate Journey of Self-Acceptance

Christopher L. Heuertz

For the Enneagram enthusiast looking to deepen their transformation, *The Enneagram of Belonging* offers an enlightening, enriching path forward.

Many have discovered the Enneagram to be a powerful tool for self-understanding, yet knowing ourselves doesn't necessarily mean we accept ourselves. Most of us tend to curate the personality of our type: leading with the traits we perceive as positive and sidelining the traits that cause us shame.

But what if it all belonged? Rather than furthering our own fragmentation, what if we dared to make peace with the whole of who we are with bold compassion? *The Enneagram of Belonging* is your guide to this essential journey.

While most contemporary Enneagram books stop at the descriptions of the nine types, Enneagram teacher and *The Sacred Enneagram* bestselling author Chris Heuertz uncovers the missing link in our journey of living into our true self: radical self-compassion that can bring us back to belonging.

Rather than get stuck on stereotypes or curated personality, Heuertz proposes we develop an honest relationship with our type, confronting our "inner dragons," practicing self-compassion, and thereby coming to fully belong to ourselves—and, ultimately, to love itself.

In this in-depth examination of the Enneagram of Personality, you will discover:

- A fresh, compassionate way of understanding your childhood wound, which Heuertz reframes as your Kidlife Crisis
- Your unique subtype and how this colors your dominant type, plus how to work with your Enneagram instinct
- Practical insight to help you find freedom from your type's Passions and Fixations
- Your personalized path back to belonging, as you come home to your true self
- . . . and much more.

Also available: *The Enneagram of Belonging Workbook.*

Available in stores and online!